EXTRAORDINARY DESIRE TO WIN

EXTRAORDINARY DESIRE TO WIN

Zeenat Ara

PRABHAT
PRAKASHAN

Published by
PRABHAT PRAKASHAN PVT. LTD.
4/19 Asaf Ali Road,
New Delhi-110 002 (INDIA)
e-mail: prabhatbooks@gmail.com

ISBN 978-93-5266-044-5
EXTRAORDINARY DESIRE TO WIN
by Zeenat Ara

Edition
2026

Paperback Price
₹ 500.00 (Rupees Five Hundred only)

Printed at
Jai Laxmi Printing Press, Delhi

I want to dedicate this book to all those people
Who want to win all odds of their life, with smile
On their face, one who never blame or cry for with
They are blessed, instead show their happiness for
Being chosen by god to learn from the most difficult Test.

Author's Note

I had been confined to my bed for most of my life because of a curvature in my back (in medical terms 'scoliosis'). Some people, who come to meet me, both relatives and friends, generally show their sympathy and feel sorry for my being in this terrible condition and blame Allah (God) that He has been partial to me, making my life worthless as compared to the so-called normal people.

And during my small conversation with a limited number of words, I always fail to make them fully convinced that I do not have even the slightest of regret for how Allah has designed my life. So, I decided that I should write my autobiography through which I can give the message to the whole world: "We all should keep patience in whatever condition we are or what we may be facing, with a smile on, because it will raise the level of energy inside to overcome all odds of life and never blame God as He chooses His best warriors of all to fight the battle, in whom He has confidence that he/she will win."

- In this autobiography, I will reveal the challenges which I faced during my life so far, unknown to even around me most of the time because they always find me smiling.
- Secondly, an important objective of this book is that I want to spread awareness in India about SMA (Spinal Muscular Atrophy). Here in our country, people lack awareness about this problem, due to

which they sometimes fail to give proper care to their children in time to improve their lifespan.
And last but not the least, you will get to know how I achieved my education as a small girl withstanding all types of challenges that kept coming in my way, one after another, till class 12th, which could not be completed by the time I write this book and many more painful events of my life, with which I chose to fight without losing hope.

Acknowledgement

This book becomes a reality with the kind support and help of many individual. I would like to extend my sincere thanks to all of them.

Foremost I want to offer this endeavor to our almighty allah for the wisdom he bestowed upon me, the strength ,the peace of my mind and good health in order to finish this book.

I would like to express my deep gratitude to my aunt Late Ayesha Khatoon and my teacher Mrs. Negi Ma'am because of whose blessings the dream of writing this book became true.

I would also like to acknowledge the help provided by Mr. N.P. Singh (D.M. of Noida) who willingly gave his precious time to encourage me to start the work, persever with it and finally to publish it and also gave full health support time to time. He was like a back bone to me through out the journey and helped me in overcoming the various obsticles which came on my way while the journey of writing this book.

I am also thankful to Ar Sangeeta Aggarwal and Mrs. Arti Marwah for her valuable and constructive suggestions in molding this book into a more interesting book.

My thanks and appreciation also go to Ponty Chaddha Foundation and Dr. Vandana Sharma (Director of MBCN) who initially recognized my talent and put forward to the whole world.

I would like to express my gratitude towards my family for the encouragement which helped me in completion of this book. My beloved and supportive parents (Dr. Jamal Ahmed and Rizwana Khatoon) and my sibblings (Ar Mazhar Husain and Er Erum Fatima). They all always have been by my side when times I needed them the most.

I am also thankful to all my friends and Doctors who have willingly helped me out with their abilities.

Thanks,

Zeenat Ara

Why This Book

I am Zeenat Ara and I am going to take you to the world of a beautiful girl. She was living in a world which she had never expected for herself, same as we people think that we deserve the best, she also expected the same, but it was entirely different from her imagination.

She was going through a life which was totally different from others, very challenging and full of obstacles. In spite of all these hurdles, she had to continue living. She never took her life so hard, instead she would say, "If Allah (God) had not chosen me to take birth with this problem, life would not have been so interesting."

Actually, she loved to face the challenges and it was her whole life's challenge which left her with no option but to live. Thus, she decided she would only pay attention on the positivity around her and always try to improve negativities in her life.

The excitement comes with the thought of visualising the real picture of that amazing girl. However, I may not be able to describe that girl exactly in words, but I am sure if some day you would get a chance to meet her, you would be able to believe that a real fighter exists on this very earth.

She was not a simple girl, instead she was a very different and interesting girl. She believed in living life to the fullest and never let a single moment go waste without enjoying it.

Suffering with disability (SMA) in which she couldn't do anything of her own, except thinking and speaking, just like babies, you must have seen, who are dependent on their mothers for all their necessities. She was also dependent on others, but she never let her disability come into her way to happiness.

But that doesn't mean her life was not tough, you and I cannot imagine her pain even in dream, for that we need to collect all humans' courage on this earth. Only she herself and God could feel the pain behind her smiling face.

She herself didn't know that God had at least spent some time in creating and developing her into a beautiful girl. She never noticed her beauty. However, later on, she got to know about this from others. People praised and admired her, which made her to believe that she happened to be one amongst the most beautiful people. I can say she was like a red rose whom God has permeated with strength like that of the rose which is filled with beautiful fragrance. She always blushed like the red rose spreading its soothing smell all around. Her beauty was not only external, rather she was more beautiful from the inside, in her heart, which would reflect radiantly from her face.

I suppose, by now, your curiosity to know that girl must have increased greatly as I have compared her with the queen of flowers, rose. So, now I am not going to take much of your time to disclose all about her. Just close your eyes and feel this girl.

Contents

1
Zeenat, God's Gift to this World!

She had very fine features: big eyes with a rosy shining over the eyelids, which do not require any man-made assistance over it, fine eyebrows which never arise any need of a beautician and a straight nose just like that of a Barbie doll that never cultivates in her a desire to apply any external material to make it look straight, and dark dense shining hair. Such hair is generally a dream of almost all girls. Her lips were very fine, just like flower petals that, whenever she smiled, seemed like a shower of flowers. Her feet were so sweet that once one of her cousins Zainab gave her a compliment, "Never ever keep your legs on earth, lest they become dirty." And it came true that her legs never touched the earth even at the time when she deeply wanted to do that. And her skin was fair; not very fair, not very light, it was the best. Such complexion is rarely found in people.

So, that was her description. You must have fancied a real Zeenat in your imagination.

Now again you must have got confused why I am taking my name in place of that girl. You are absolutely right. This is my world. I have taken you into my own world to feel my life's experiences.

You might not be interested in exploring the life of an ordinary girl. Why would it matter to you if she had gone through the toughest time with a smile on, as she did not want to spoil the surroundings around her by showing her

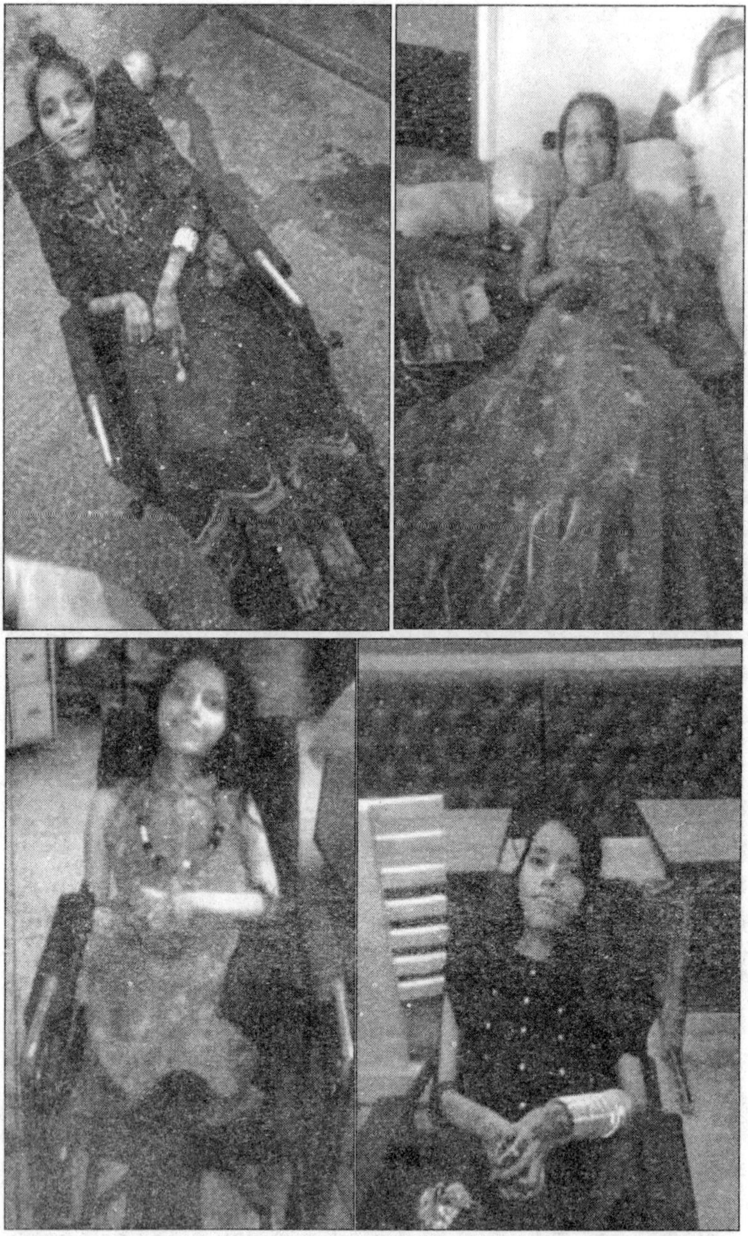

Glimpses of Zeenat.

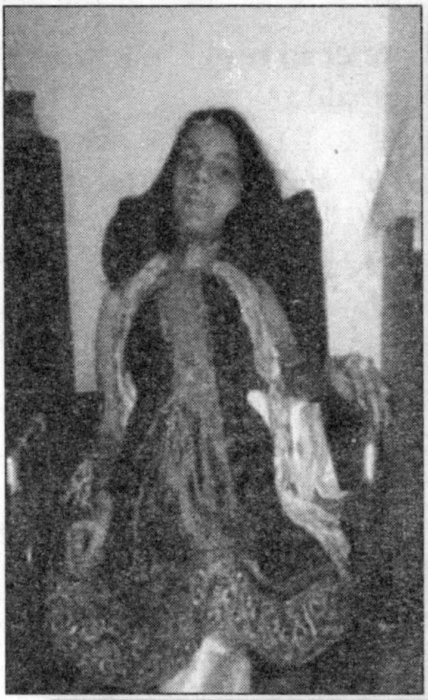

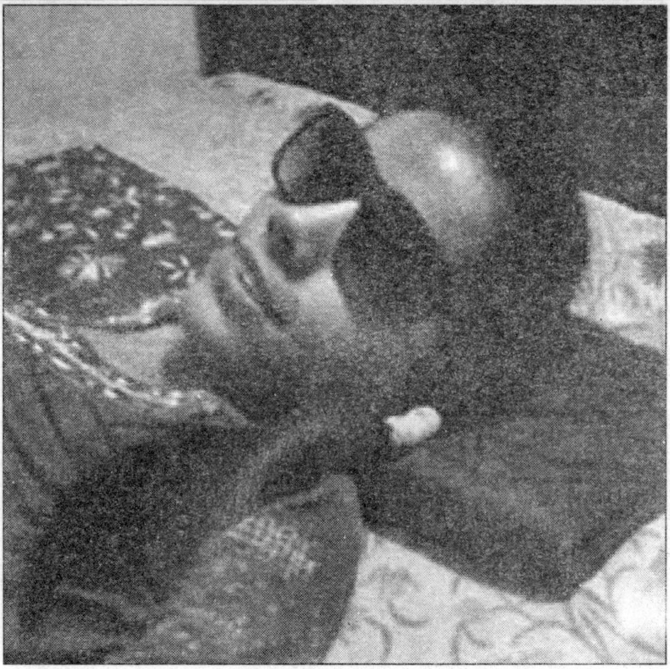

Glimpses of Zeenat.

pain to all? Instead you would prefer to read the ups and downs in the lives of famous personalities.

Yes, I am that beautiful girl and I am not popular like a celebrity or a freedom fighter, and this is a message from a real person to this world. I want you to be aware of people having SMA (spinal muscular atrophy) and the limitations it causes to people with the passage of time. I make a request – just encourage these people towards the betterment of life as well as help them proceed towards living an independent life.

□

2

The Story of Real Fighter: Zeenat Ara

I was born on 18.4.1987; to my parents I brought a lot of luck. My father started getting various job opportunities and soon they shifted from Kanpur to Gurgaon. With this, we went one step ahead in life. My father could provide much better education to my siblings as this town in the NCR were developing well in that period. After we shifted there, in nearly 10 years, it has almost changed entirely.

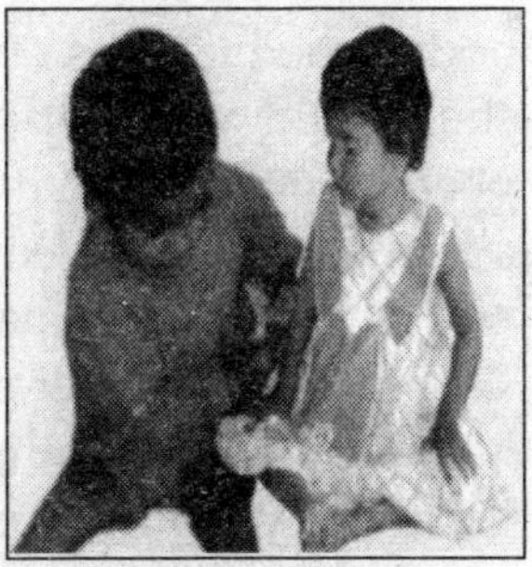

Little Zeenat with her younger brother Mazhar.

We moved there because my father, Jamal Ahmed got a job in the same city and worked in SHAW WALLACE. However, four years later, we shifted to Noida.

We are a family of seven members: father Jamal, mother Rizwana Khatoon, and three siblings – elder brother Azher Husain, younger brother Mazhar Husain and sister Erum Fatima. She was the youngest. My father's sister or Bua, Aisha was also living with us. In fact, she formed the most important part of my life. You must know about her as an individual before knowing her contribution in my life.

She had devoted all her life towards bringing up my father and after my birth, she decided that she would make use of her remaining life by keeping herself busy with me.

So, she spent all her life's valuable moments in caring as well as looking after me.

She was a lady who never lived her life for herself; rather she preferred to render service to others. Whether they were our relatives, friends or others, she would offer her service to all and make them feel comfortable.

Now let's come to her contribution in my life. You could not have believed that I could not think of a moment without her. She was myoxygen.

I was very close to her and she took good care of mine. I could not sleep if she was not sleeping next to me. Since my body ached if I was remained in one position continuously, she would wake up at frequent intervals to change my position, whenever it was required. She fed me, gave me a bath, made me sleep comfortably, and so on. In simple words, you can say that all my daily tasks were done by her. This made my father concentrate on his professional life as he had to go to another city every week. It was part of his job and my mother could attend to other children fully.

□

3
Desire to be Educated Like Others

My other siblings would go to school everyday and then come back home with a burden of homework that was needed to be completed the day before they went to school again. This daily routine would motivate to do the same. But being a small girl, at the age of 8-9 years, I couldn't realize that it was my right to go to school and study like others. I would think that going to school wouldn't be easy for me, as I didn't have the strength required by people to go to school everyday.

I felt I wouldn't be able to sit for four to five hours with normal children because I possessed the least balance in my body. But the motivation of being an educated girl didn't leave my mind. I started studying on my own. I used to read my siblings' books and then would practice writing in a notebook. Sometimes when my cousin Hena, who lived a few km away from my home, would visit me in weekends, we both used to play teacher-teacher. In our game, she would teach me all what she had learnt during her classes at school. That way I would get a chance to collect more information and the level of my knowledge improved.

I should share with you an event of my life. When the desire for education increased in me, I got to know its importance in life too.

It was a time when I was around 7 years old. I was very happy because I was expecting Hena, my cousin's visit in two days. She was my Mama's (mother's brother) daughter. I used to feel very happy in her company as I would get a chance to study and learn more interesting things, about which I would have known little before she started visiting and teaching me. She was a very good pretender. She would imitate her teachers, like most children do at this age, and then copy them accordingly.

The day came and this time she taught me names of the capitals of countries. I found this topic very interesting. I verbally learnt five or six names in one night of her stay and wanted to learn more, but unfortunately, she had to leave early next morning as she had to attend school.

I felt bad within and thought if I too would have been a school-going girl, I would not have needed her because I could have known the names of more capitals, maybe more than she knew.

So, this was the realization about importance of education, although it's very difficult to make ourselves understand things when we are small children.

Days went by and I kept myself busy with reading my siblings' books and practicing them in a notebook.

□

4

I Continued to Make an Effort to Educate Myself

As a child, I realized the vast difference between me and other children. I can't explain how difficult it had been for me to accept this ten-digit word *difference*. It was like a gap that did not practically seem to be bridged. There were many more limitations in my life as compared to others, which kept convinced me to believe that I can't get all the rights which normal human beings are supposed to have.

It was what this world was bent upon making me believe but my eyes never responded to it. Somewhere in my heart, I felt that I was equally strong from the inside, although I happened to be physically slightly different from those so-called normal people, and my feelings, my desires, my aspirations were all same.

And do you know this is a truth – your eyes speak what your heart says? Our heart has a direct connection with our eyes.

So there was a person, who lived with us, named Farhan. I called him Mamu (Uncle). I don't know what, but maybe he saw something in my eyes, a desire for education. I am so much fond of studies that all the time I had a pen and paper in my hands and so I used to write something or the other all the time.

One day, I was sitting in my drawing room, my back leaning against the wall, when he came and sat next to me. He was holding some nursery-level books in his hands.

He said, "What are you writing? See what I have brought for you."

I looked; there were books. It was like receiving a treasure. He said, "These books will be with me. I will teach you everyday after I return from office." When he said that, I didn't like it, because I wanted to have those books with me and study them myself even when he was not there, but he didn't give me because he thought I might tear the books since I was still a small child.

At that time, I had this feeling how he could be my teacher because teachers never keep books of children at the time when the school bell rings. My siblings would always bring their books back from school.

I felt very bad as I wanted to have proper education like normal people. I wanted to give exams on a particular date, same as my siblings used to do, but nothing like that was to happen in my case, that uncle would not have been able to give me proper time. He used to teach me whenever he would get time.

This world made all its effort to make me believe that there is a vast difference between me and others, but my heart was never ready to accept what this world wanted to make me believe.

There were tears in my eyes when I saw children of my age going to school. I would expect in my heart that someday somebody would definitely help me overcome this distance created by the worldly people between me and others.

And it was Allah, who would always show the worldly people that he created everyone of the same level, although in his physical design, he may have made some people different from others, but he made them equally strong and capable from the inside.

□

5

Finally a Big Change in My Life

Studying from home didn't seem good to me because I was unable to clear all my doubts and it was true one can't study without proper guidance sitting at home, especially when it is the initial point, one needs proper coaching or schooling.

This resulted in my loneliness. I felt like crying all the time, since I was very young but I couldn't explain my feelings to others. I used to think how people will help me when I can't even sit myself, take out my books from my bag, can't hold my neck firm. Which school will take me in then? I would always sit alone, rarely talk to others, but, my hopes were always high. There was always a feeling in my heart that I would win.

When my mother saw all this, she felt bad from within and had the feeling that she was not turning out to be a good mother and that very moment, she decided that she would send me to some school soon. In any case, she was not bold enough like other women but she tried her best and found out that there are some special schools in Delhi, where she could send me, but the problem remained who would take me to Delhi everyday as my father was out of station for most of the time.

She was a mother. She had kept me in her womb for nine months. So, she was the only one who could hear my silent voice. She got to know what could bring her daughter's smile back.

And to bring that smile back, she again made a search and found out an aunt's son, who was living in the same locality in which we were living, going to a special school because he was having some mental issues. So, my mother decided to send me to the same school as it provided education to physically challenged children till class 5th.

She met aunty Jasvant Kaur who happened to be a very helpful lady. Whenever she would find me at home, she would ask my mother to take me out. If not possible, then at least in the evening. For that, she even offered her son's wheelchair, but that was not an issue. It was my home, which was located upstairs.

The staircase also brought limitations to my life. I would rarely go downstairs. Whenever it was very urgent, my mother or other family members would bring me down the floor, like when I got ill or when I needed a doctor's attention at once, or when my family members were going to meet some relatives, friends and the like.

I remember an incident when these stairs had become a big hurdle between me and my happiness. It was a time when my cousin Hena (my Mama's daughter) had come to my home with her family on a weekend. We all were of the same age: her siblings and my siblings. We were playing; we played in whatever free time we got. We never let it go waste.

So, in the evening, she asked me, "Manni, today we will play in the nearby park. It will be fun."

Manni is my nickname, my family members call me by this name.

I said: "Yes, we will get our dolls married."

My mother came and said, "Children, go and play outside."

Hena said, "Fufi, we will take Manni along."

At this, my mother said, "You all go first and take Manni's chair along. I am bringing her in a while."

All the children went down and I was lying down in the drawing room; lights were off as it was the evening time, the dim natural light was coming through the window next to the bed I was laying. That very moment, I was lost in a thought. I couldn't feel what was going around me. Actually I was hurt immensely and realized my limitation. I thought why I didn't go with them.

When I think about that moment now, I feel as if I were there as I am today. I could better make myself understand that situation.

My mother met Jasvant aunty and asked her about the school and requested her to go with her for the admission. In a few days, both of them went to the school and secured my admission. The principal was so impressed to see my desire for education.

□

6

A Step Taken Towards New Life

A step was already taken by my mother towards a new life, which enhanced the beauty of the most beautiful girl, because now my lips learnt to smile more often. I got what my heart was crying for since a long time.

Now, in the year 1994, I started going to school regularly and that was the reason behind my smile. At that time, I was 8 years old, my mother and my father's sister Aisha, both would prepare me for school everyday with their combined effort.

That school was a small NGO and was located at Sector 40, Noida, at a small distance from my home. Its name was INTERACT SOCIETY.

Zeenat with her mother Rizwana Khatoon and Principal Mrs. Burman in the year 1994.

At school, all my arrangements were made by my principal, Mrs. Burman. She took help from the physiotherapist in making my sitting arrangement because I required special attention to keep my posture in the correct position.

The physiotherapist, Anjali Didi used pillows and made me sit in a CP chair, which had a neck rest attached to it. Although that chair was hard as it was made up of wood but was better than a normal one.

I felt as if in another world full of people chattering, sharing one another's point of view. I was unable to believe that the world could be so colourful.

Here I related the world with the word colourful. What I mean to say was that the world is colourful because I got to meet people with different desires, attitudes and capabilities, and the most important thing was competition. I saw in everyone's eyes the spark of competition to become the best in life.

Before joining the school, my home was the entire world for me and the limited number of people living in it were my companions, but with joining this school, the concept of the world had been expanded in my mind and it also made me believe that the world is full of magic and it helped in developing the confidence in me to live in this magical world, so that I could get all in my life I had been sacrificing. I was very happy because now I was getting proper attention from the teachers. Now I didn't require to request anyone at home to teach me, besides this I had the opportunity to interact with more people, more than what I expected.

All these changes came out wonderful to me.

□

7

My Name Zeenat Ara Turned Out to be Very Lucky for My Family

A big thing had happened in my life which made my family members believe that I was not an ordinary girl but much more than that, maybe a blessing from God and they started considering me as a God's gift.

Here I do not mean to say that with this event in my life, they (my parents) started loving me more than they used to, their love for me was always priceless, rather they believed in God's blessing being with me, and He would never be partial with their girl when compared with other normal humans. They believed God is always there with their child in all ups and downs of life.

This change came when one of my siblings put my name in all pages of tickets, which they used to be given by their school every year at the time of fiesta. The school would hold a lucky draw at the end of the fiesta. The person whose name would be drawn first would be honoured by a big prize. And I won it.

My siblings went to the fiesta on the scheduled date and came back early without listening to the announcement, which was about to be made by a teacher any moment then. They left the venue since they were firm that they were not going to win the opportunity.

Next day, when my elder brother (Azhar Husain) entered his class, there was some fuss going all around that he had won the first prize in lucky draw in his sister's name 'Zeenat'. He couldn't believe in the spreading news.

That day he went home happily and the moment he reached home, he let others know about this news. When everyone listened to this news, they embraced me.

After a while, when all folks released me from their embrace. I thought with wide open eyes what had happened. I thought as if I were going to learn walking in the coming days. This thought came to my mind because it was the only biggest thing that could have happened in my life.

What could a ten-year-old girl have hoped for more than that?

Zeenat with her father Jamal Ahmad receiving the first prize from the principal of Vishwa Bharti Public School, Noida in 1995 after the fiesta.

The true or real picture of happiness was seen in my family, when I was taken by my father and one of my cousins named Attaullah to my sibling's school to receive the prize, they were so happy to bring the prize as soon as possible.

As I entered the big gate, I couldn't believe my eyes. I never expected any school could have such a big gate or was provided with unlimited space. This thought took place in my mind because the school in which I took admission recently was even less than one-fourth of that.

My cousin, who was holding me, stepped in the office, the room was so wide that all children of my school could have settled in the principal's office, although I don't remember his name. He offered us to sit in a big soothing couch, my father and he talked for some time together. Then he asked to click a photo with me. For that he took my hold from my cousin. He was so old that while holding me in his lap, his body seemed to be bending to a side, and I had a fear of falling down from his grip. During this, he had given me a compliment which is still vivid as a spoken voice in my mind. He said, "One day, she will become a queen and will rule over the millions of hearts." He said so while staring deep inside my eyes. Soon after, we left with the prize.

□

8

A Special Meeting

As I have told you, the most desirable thing in my life was 'education', which now seemed to be fulfilled. And things were going smoothly. After some time, a teacher named Mrs. Negi, who had joined this school for her daughter, Bharti Didi, who was also suffering with mental issues, came to me and got me shifted to her own class. Before joining this school, she was in a normal school. Here in this special school, she used to take senior students like those of the third, fourth and fifth standards. There were no classes beyond these grades.

Mrs. Negi Ma'am had been watching me since the day she had joined the school. She understood my capacity in one go and directly went to the principal for permission to shift me to her class.

As soon as she got the permission, she started teaching me. She saw a spark in my eyes, a desire to be like others and saw something in me, which made me superior to others and it was my positive attitude towards life what impressed her. I would never take my life as very tough, instead I would take out the toughest from my life and prefer to live it with a big smile on my face.

I also enjoyed being taught by her. Her method of teaching was the same as in a normal school. So, it was my requirement. What difference I found in the school was that all children were following different syllabi due to their unmatchable levels. Mrs. Negi Ma'am was trying her best to keep up with all children's requirement, due to which sometimes my studies got delayed and I would feel very irritated because I wanted to complete my syllabus as soon as possible.

Later, with more understanding, I found out the level of education I always expected to have, I was not getting in this special school. There was a vast difference in the level of teaching between my school and the normal school. But I couldn't do anything in it because something is better than nothing and if a person has faith, he or she can turn that something into everything in no time. So, I followed this with patience.

My brain and heart were functioning normally. It was getting fresher and brighter by the time I was entering into adulthood. It was only my physical body that forced me to become the part of a special school; otherwise I would have taken admission in a normal school. The problem was I could not hold my neck in place or move myself an inch if needed. There was the least balance in my body. My physical condition wasn't like that I could sit for longer period of time in a class in normal school and could follow instructions given by teachers, I was needed an attendant all the time who could make notes on my behalf but no such facilities were available in normal schools. It was like my desire of getting proper education doesn't make any sense to the people because my physical condition doesn't fit to their criteria. But this is wrong all schools should have the facilities for children with less nobility. There should be some separate provisions for such children who have deserve for education but could not make it due to physical condition, Infact govt. should make provision regarding this and make compulsory to open a section for such children in all govt. schools and colleges so that people like us don't suffer in future.

So, this unpredictable meeting with Mrs. Negi Ma'am gave a new direction to my life.

□

9

A New Member Came in My Life

By the time I was 10 years old, my mother gave birth to a boy. He was very sweet. He had very sharp features, and due to his fluffy or dense eyelid, he resembled more like a rabbit.

My siblings and I usually were fascinated to see babies of our relatives and family friends. So, the entry of that new member brought happiness and celebration in my family as well as in my life because I already had immense love for children below my age. Now, with this, one can imagine the degree of happiness in my life with the entry of that little prince.

I had many relatives and family friends, who had small kids. So, whenever they visited me during vacations or on other occasions, I would ask them to keep their babies in my lap and when they put them in my lap, I would talk to them and would prefer to play with them all the time.

I loved that newborn baby so much that if any member from my family would go against my will, I would shout or show annoyance, but it wasn't so in his case. I could tolerate any limit if it came to that baby. He could sit on my head, pull my hair hard. In simple words, he could do anything to me but I never said a word to him for all those acts. Rather I would make him sleep over me, put him on my legs with the help of my mother, so that he could feel he was on a swing.

Doing all this sometimes caused me pain in my abdomen but it was a small thing against my little brother's happiness.

I remember an incident through which you could be able to know how important he was to me.

When he grew a little older, he became fond of cars. He used to sit on beds and ask Mummy to give him a plate. When Mummy gave him a plate, he used to play with it as if he were running a car by holding it in his hands in the form of a car steering.

He would never play with soft toys like teddy-bears, dolls, etc. And that was the reason I also never presented him with these types of gifts. What would happen, every year on his birthday we (my siblings) would collect our savings and buy sweets and cars and then celebrate his birthday.

He loved to play with cars as much as that, after some period, he developed a habit of playing car on the floor. He would ask Mummy to lay him down on the floor and then laying on the floor, he would run the car making a sound [*dhoon dhoon dhoon*]. When I realized his new habit, I feared ants could enter his ears and since he was a small baby, he would not have been able to explain the reason behind his pain in his ears in case any insect entered his ears.

I knew of my limitation. That is why I compared myself with a baby. I knew he wouldn't be able to keep himself away from the thing that was supposed to hurt him. Another thing in his case was that if he saw something coming near to him and that could hurt him, he would not shout, until it actually hurt him. Because of this, many a time, I asked Mummy not to lay him down on the floor.

But Mummy would always take it lightly. Her point of view was simple. She was also right that babies should be developed strongly in odd conditions.

When she completely stopped giving importance to my words, my fear for him increased much more and I decided that I will do something myself, although it wasn't easy for me to help someone physically, because when you are already dependent on others for your basic needs, what help you could provide others?

But believe me, when your brain and heart are working properly, you could bring any impossible height beneath your feet. Always remember, your brain is the master of your entire body. You should always keep it active.

So, I did. I said to my aunty (Aisha), "Please lay me down on the floor as well." In that way, I could keep an eye on my brother's activity. If any dangerous thing would come near him, I could at least shout for help. In this way, I would have been satisfied that he is not hurt by any insect on the floor.

□

10

Knew the Exact Meaning of Friendship

When I was 12 years old when Buti had this feeling. Whatever it was, it brought excitement and curiosity in my life.

Whenever I would see my siblings going around children of their age, talk about them with me, and share the happening of events with each other (with their friends) like events in classroom as well as at park where they used to play. This would make me put pressure on my mind and make me think: 'What is this relationship? Why don't I have such pleasure in my life as well?'

I know by now you must be thinking what a foolish girl I had been when I don't know what this relationship called 'friendship' is. You are absolutely right; anybody in your place must have thought that way. But then, I will say: Keep your eyes close and think. Suppose a girl who had no friends and, at the same time, she sees other people have many of them and they have lots of things in common to talk over and this girl extended her hand to make one of those as her friend and then what she would get in return. Nothing. They will expect her to come up to their requirements, like they will expect her to go to the park and play with them. Wherever they wish her to go, she will have to be there.

Now can you imagine that this girl will have the feeling that she is alone and would expect to have the same pleasure in her life as well? How could you then expect of her that she should know the meaning of this relationship called 'friendship',when nobody prefers to create such relationship with her? She will only have the pain in her heart, which she can only feel but can't show it to others.

Nothing is in the hands of anybody except God. This was my belief and the same did happen. God (Allah) sent a pretty girl as my friend in my recently joined school. Her name was Ranjana Gupta. She was very beautiful. When I met her first at school, I could not believe my eyes that another beautiful girl exists on this earth as I earlier believed that I was the most beautiful girl of all.

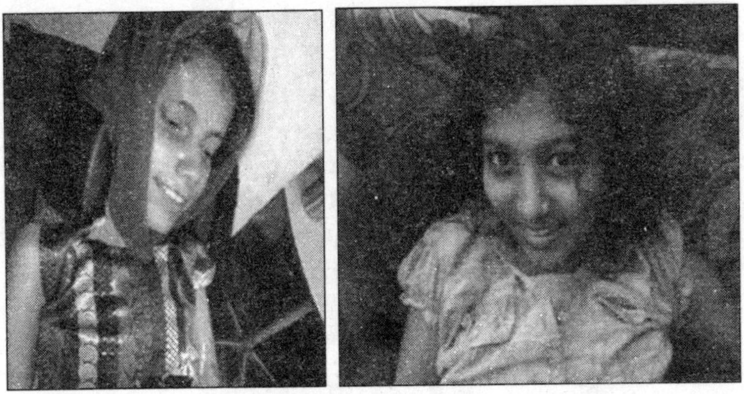

Zeenat and her friend Ranjana Gupta.

Two Resembling Faces

When we both came in contact with each other, she told me everything about herself and asked me about my life and everything. She was just like an angel who entered my life with open feathers and filled it with bright light of happiness. She was like my replica. The only difference between both of us was she had a dull skin complexion and mine was fair.

In normal course, what happens is that a beautiful girl is jealous of another beautiful girl, but we had no such feelings. I never had that feeling, nor did she.

I never felt jealous of her because you feel jealous when you have fear of being beaten by someone.

But truly there was no such competition between us. Rather, we both appreciated each other for our best work.

When I saw her first, one thing came to my mind that she also had the same problem which I was suffering from. This thought rose in me because she had many similarities with me, like she used to sit in the same CP chair I used to, she had the same writing frequency and, the most important, her brain acted the same as mine. We had many similarities which I didn't find in any student at my school. That might be the reason why I thought she had the same problem like that of mine, but later on in life, I got to know she had JAPANESE ENCEPHALITIS which is a mosquito-borne viral infection, which leads to inflammation, irritation and swelling of the brain. Because of this infection, a patient may go in coma and later when he comes out of it, sometimes he may lose the power of walking, standing and other movements. But the patient having this problem does not require much care later in life as in SMA because in SMA, it creates many health complications, which threatens even life of the patient about which I will tell you later.

So, the entry of this girl in my life provided me with the opportunity of having the pleasure of a true friend, thereby knowing the exact meaning of this relationship – *friendship*.

□

11
Image of a Mother

As I have told you, I had to join a special school due to my numerous limitations. I needed one's attention all the time in case I lost control of my neck. It may fall down or I may need to change my permanent position frequently.

Actually, first I would try to change my position by myself so that I could get some relief but after putting my best effort, if I was unable to move my limbs and if in that case it starts aching, I would require someone's help.

You can imagine how difficult it becomes when you know the reason behind your pain but you become helpless because of your inability to move your limbs.

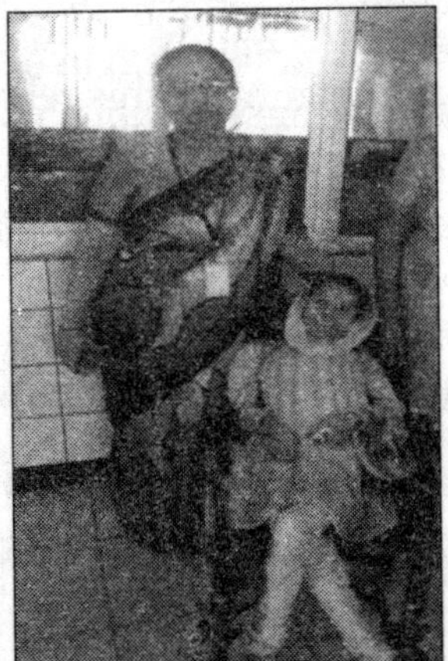

Zeenat with Vice Principal Mrs. Saraswati Negi at MBCN School.

The school in which I used to go had a good caring facility. My class teacher, Mrs. Negi cares for me a lot. She never takes help from any attendant even if I need to go to washroom or when the attendant is busy in serving other children. She never waited for her to get free and feed me. She would herself do it.

I remember an incident when I saw the image of my mother in her, although it is irrelevant to relate any second person with a mother because you can get a replacement for anything on earth except your biological mother. It is the most precious gift by God to us. We can't reciprocate the work done by a mother for us. It will always be more than the work done by us to her.

Now coming to the main point as I was telling you, I saw the image of my mother in Mrs. Negi. Actually what had happened, one day I went to school with a sore throat and then suddenly I started coughing during the class severely. That happened because of the accumulated cough which kept on forming secretions but couldn't come out due to my inability to spit out forcefully because of weakness.

When my teacher Mrs. Negi Ma'am saw me having difficulty in coughing, she went ahead leaving other children aside, took me in her lap, lowered me downward and put her finger inside my mouth in order to bring out all cough and I could feel relief only then.

This act I could only expect of my mother or someone very close to me like my siblings as well as my very close relatives in a rare case. But in actual life, you sometimes do not come close to each other by blood relation alone. Rather with the strong attraction between two hearts, the same attraction I felt for Mrs. Negi Ma'am.

□

12

A Shock that Shattered Me

My youngest brother, who had been born after a long time, later named Saif Husain, was suffering from the same problem I had (SMA type 1). He was diagnosed within three months of his birth but I didn't know about it at the time that he was so diagnosed. I was too young to know about it. My parents didn't tell me because I was very young, and so, they thought it might bring me in a state of big shock. However, later on, with the passage of time, his activities decreased day by day. That made me put my queries to my elders. When they let me know about the truth, I felt shattered within me.

I cannot explain my feeling about that moment. There was darkness around my eyes. I felt as if my life had been recreated with more challenges, and the person who was going to face it was more important than I was for myself. I knew how difficult it happens to make a child understand himself that he can't get all the pleasure of life due to his problem, when he sees other children going to school, playing and enjoying life in all possible ways they feel like.

I didn't want to see that pain in my brother's eyes, but I couldn't do anything. I have never blamed my own disability, I never got hurt so much when I saw my desires being suppressed due to my helplessness in all my life till then.

Since the day I knew about this news, I would remain upset and started noticing my brother Saif.

One day I noticed a girl, 4 years younger than him, living next to my home, who used to come to my place everyday, came and then started running all over the house. At seeing this, my brother suddenly became quiet. The disappointment of not being able to do so could be seen in his eyes, but neither I could explain him the reason nor he could ask me for it because he himself was not in a position to make out the reasons. He was just 6 years old. What a small baby could have thought of, he was only confused about all these things!

That day and the whole night I kept crying and asked Allah (God) why he did so with my brother also. I was very tense and oppressed that night, that my tears were not stopping from coming down from my eyes. I was in the biggest pain of my life. Even in my own disability, I never got hurt so much when I see my desires being suppressed due to my disability, but when I saw my brother in the same situation, I couldn't bear it. It felt like somebody had separated my heart from my body.

Can you imagine a life without it? If there is no heart in your body, there will be no feeling. I lived many months with no feeling in my body after that incident. But I kept patience with the belief that it was a test by Allah, the owner of this world for me, and the real winner is the one who wins the test given by the owner of this world and I wanted to win that test by keeping patience.

□

13

School Services Turned Bad from Good

Now under Mrs. Negi Ma'am's supervision, I had completed the 5th class. She used to teach me in the same way as was done in normal schools; on the other side, in special schools, teachers need not have degrees. They are only required to do a course known as special education because they need not teach children in classes, they only teach them mannerisms, but this was not in my case. My requirements were different. They were like those of normal children and that was noticed by Mrs. Negi Ma'am. So, immediately she changed her method of teaching to normal.

I was very happy with the way I was being taught. My studies got disturbed when Mrs. Negi Ma'am resigned and left the school. Initially, it became very difficult for me to adjust myself with other teachers present there. They were not that expert in understanding my requirements, like they didn't know in what position my neck should be kept so that I feel comfortable while studying, in what intervals of time I need to change the positions of my legs, etc. There were so many things they took time to learn. Even then they did not become that efficient as Mrs. Negi Ma'am had been.

I would have left that school the very next day after Mrs. Negi Ma'am submitted her resignation, but during that period, that school was nearest to my home, my mother said that I should continue going to the same school as I could reach home within 20 minutes of school bell. She said so because I used to get tired being in bus for long hours.

Later, with the passage of time, I got myself adjusted as the school authorities changed many teachers as per my comfort because they were afraid that if they didn't do so, I might leave their school. They had very few children at that time, maybe around 100.

Everything went well for two years. They provided good teachers who were not only special educators but also B.Sc., M.Sc., as they knew I could leave their school any time and they didn't want to lose a good student who could bring laurels to their school.

Later, after two-three years, their service became bad from good. I don't know the reason behind this as usually these things are understood by school administration better.

They started providing me teachers who were all simple and special educators and were unable to teach me properly.

A special educator is the one who has specialised in teaching children requiring special assistance in understanding things like children who have mental disability. But in my case, I had a physical problem and not a mental problem, due to which I was facing a problem with those teachers.

Here my intention is not to hurt any special educators. I just want to explain that the school provided me teachers later. They were all simple and special educators and they used to try their best to keep up to my requirements but many times they lacked the capacity to give full explanation I required.

□

14

Lost the Most Precious Thing in My Life

After two-three years got over smoothly, a big tragedy happened in my life, which weakened me more from the inside. It was when my brother Saif was not going well due to constant respiratory infection.

When I would see my brother in pain, I would become nervous and wish to get all his suffering and give him my health.

But since at this point, we people become helpless, we are left with nothing in our hands as over these things only, our creator Allah has control. We can only ask him and if he answered to our prayers, that means we are among his favourites.

I prayed to Him every second as well as tried to find out the reason why that was happening to my brother but I didn't get any answers. That was so, maybe because I myself was very young at that time, maybe around 15 years old, and didn't have much knowledge about what exactly could be the reason behind my brother's suffering. Even my family didn't have the slightest idea.

Actually, he was getting frequent respiratory infections because of his inborn disease SMA type 1 (spinal muscular atrophy). It is found to be severe than all SMA types in which lungs' muscles become weak and don't function as in normal children, which causes frequent respiratory infection in early childhood, about which my family didn't know and they provided him with normal medication.

Later, when they took him to the Kalawati hospital, he took his last breath and left this mortal world peacefully.

Soon after, a person, known to my father who was very much responsible for deterioration of my brothers condition just because my father trusted him a lot and followed his advice blindly, came to my home while my parents were at hospital, directly gave us this news (my siblings and me). He didn't even think at once what would be its consequences on the children. He turned out to be such a rude person who had a heart of stone.

I still remember his lines when I tried to investigate from him about my brother's health. He said, "The story of Saif is over now." This line hit me so hard that I felt like somebody had shot an arrow into my heart and it was broken into two pieces. All of us (my siblings) burst into tears and that person sitting on couch enjoyed it.

How could someone be so cruel, he didn't even think at once of making us feel calm? I know by now you all must have wanted to know his role in my life? So, I will just tell you that in everyone's life, there are people who do not leave their good impact. There might be persons who leave their negative impact. It has happened with me. He left with his negative impact on my life.

Whatever had happened with my brother, I will blame it to the doctors also at some extent. At the time of his birth at Kilash Hospital, Noida, the doctor who diagnosed him SMA, should make awake my parents about its hazardous consequences of this deadly disease latter in life. They should have guided them step by step and warn them it they don't follow it they may lose their child anytime. I know my father should have enquired about this disease himself from the doctors and should approach many more neurologist to go into the depth of this disease but he didn't being a Ph.D. but atleast doctor should have warned him and guided him ones because its their duty to guide their patients and save life. They are not supposed to opt for medical just to make money but more to save humanity. They should alteast respect the oath they are made to take at the time of getting their degree, there I am not criticizing all doctor many are so great and many are not exceptions and there in all fields but according to me in this field things should be leveled.

□

15
Painful Nights

From the day I lost my brother, every night I would cry and ask Allah why he had taken him away from me. Why he didn't give me strength so that I could look after him? I had the feeling of not being a good sister since then.

All night I would cry and beg of God at least to keep him in peace thereafter. I was unable to forget the pain he must have gone through during his last time. My cry was so feeble that my aunt (Bua) Aisha (father's sister), sleeping next to me, couldn't hear it.

He was so attached to me that most of the time he was found to be sleeping over my chest and, during this, both of us talked. I would teach him a poem, colours' names, shapes, etc. All those memories were intact in my mind as it was at the time when my brother was alive, his voice "Aapa, Aapa, what are you doing? What are you doing?" was echoing in my mind all the time I had been in my sense, only when I would go to sleep, that voice would burst into the earth.

Actually, what had happened, when everybody went to bed at night, Azhar (my elder brother) who was in class 10th at that time, used to study late into the night. He needed a companion, so he would keep Saif awake. By doing this, he could concentrate more on his studies. In between, Saif would try to confirm whether his sister (me) was still awake or gone to sleep, that is why he would call out, "Aapa, Aapa, are you still awake?"

From all this, you can imagine how difficult it would have been for me to get myself out of those memories. It was my God, who had given me strength to fight against the challenges that were prevailing on my way one by one.

□

16

Light of Hope Seen at Academic Front

A few months later, I sort of overcame the shock of my brother's death and I put attention towards my studies. At this time I might be 16 years old and when I noticed that I hadn't even completed class 6th till then. This made me a little irritated and I decided I would not let my studies suffer and worked hard to cope with it. I had already been separated from Mrs. Negi Ma'am 3 years ago and, since then, I had not got a proper teacher who could coach me in higher classes; for this I even complained to the owner of the school but it was no good, my studies were going as badly as they used to be.

Although my studies were not progressing well due to improper guidance or insufficient number of teachers, I didn't lose hope and did hard work to do my best in studies. I wished that Allah would definitely listen to me and all my problems would be overcome soon.

Then, in two days, I got the news that my then principal had left the school because she was pregnant. With this, a new principal took her place, that principal's name was Nandani. She turned out to be very good for me. She also observed my desire for studies and she wanted I must get the best possible coaching because she used to feel I had something in me which people don't and due to which I could achieve any impossible goal in life, even while being in that physical problem.

Mrs. Nandani Ma'am was a very self-oriented teacher. She never kept herself dependent on others (teachers) for getting anything done. Whenever she would get time from office work, she would come to my class or others' (children's classes) and start teaching herself. She taught me as well many times. Her main motive was that I should complete class 12th soon and then I could be able to reach my destination.

This happiness in my life didn't last long because Nandani Ma'am also left that school since she was ill-treated by the owner of the school.

□

17

Again A Drastic Change came in My Life

I was suffering not only due to my physical inability, but also due to the environment around me. It was not yet three years since my youngest brother's death, and now again, I got into a new situation. Now my elder brother, Azhar was diagnosed with swelling inside his brain and later with brain tumour.

You can imagine how difficult it can be when any member from your family is going through a stiff situation and, at the same time, you are not in a position to help him. I was going through the same situation. You can feel the pain in me when I would have been seeing tears in my brother's eyes about which nobody in my family knew, since Azhar never let them know that. He was mature and didn't want others get into any trouble. So, he generally tried to hide his pain from others but I was so sensitive that I noticed it.

Azhar, my brother was a very nice and intelligent boy. He was very good at studies and had won many prizes and trophies both in academics and sports. He was a star for his school and thus all his teachers and friends respected him a lot.

He never competed with his friends and those friends as well would make themselves available when he needed them. Something that was putting me into trouble more was when I would see children of my brother's age, who were not good in studies, were also taking admission, studying hard, while at that time, my brother was fighting with the disease. It was getting difficult for me to bear that pain.

I can't narrate you the situation clearly that I as well as my family went through during that period. We felt very helpless during that time because my father had to go out of the city every week as I have told you earlier. It was the part of his job and then there would be left no one at home, who could look after my brother when he needed to go to the washroom, change his clothes and the like. Out of illness, he sometimes vomited on the bed. In that case, he required someone's attention all the time. Although some of our relatives came for a few days to our support, but the biggest support we got was from Allah when He sent an angel in the form of Dadi named Daya to our Sector 37 home, where we were living, to our support. She came to know about my brother's illness through our family teacher, Santosh Jha who had taught me mathematics without fees for 3 months in class 6th.

The moment Dadi got to know about us, she directly came to my home and after collecting all information about my brother's illness, she took all responsibility. She would stay all day and night at my home, taking my brother's proper care by giving him medicines on time, feeding him and even taking him to the hospital as and when required.

One of my brother's close friend, Nitin Bhaiyas's mother, Rajni Aunty, also contributed a lot in giving support to my family. She would come straight from her office to my home and help my mother and Bua (aunt) in preparing meal as well as in feeding me. In that period, my neighbours did more than my own relatives and these neighbours include Bilkis Aunty and Ramrati Aunty as well.

This unexpected help increased my parent's strength more than before. They felt they are not alone. Allah had sent some angels in their favour. I can only tell you this much or else you would go into a big shock. It was the toughest time my family might have experienced ever.

I was so depressed that I said to Allah while praying, "Allah, let me be like this the whole of my life and please give my brother good health instead." But Allah had already planned something else and took out my brother's soul from his body within one year of his sickness.

I and my family was in a big shock initially but later accepted it as Allah's will.

□

18

One Year of Stay at Home

The school I used to go, as I earlier told you, was not turning up well. Their service started getting bad from good day by day. They were unable to provide all facilities and, after Mrs. Nandani left their school, it went from bad to worse. There was not even a capable attendant, who could take proper care of children.

The principal who came after Nandani, Mrs. Kavita, whom the school owner asked to teach me because of scarcity of teachers, used to treat me very badly. She would make me sit outside of her office and after making promise that she would attend me as soon as she was free from office work, she would never come all day (school hour), even after the school bell rang. And the next day, she usually put new excuses in front of me. With this bad treatment by the school authorities, I got irritated and asked my mother that I would not go to that school and due to which, I stayed at home for a long time.

Once two-three months got over being at home, I had the feeling of madness. It became very difficult to spend 24 hours at home without having anything in hand to do. My interaction with other people became limited to my family members only. I was seeing my future bleak.

My imagination seemed to be trapped within four walls of my room. I was gradually losing the power of imaging new things because my mind was confined within four walls of my room. I could not imagine anything more than that.

Sometimes at night, I would cry without letting others know about it.

Actually, at night, I get a chance to talk to my Allah, my creator alone without the presence of any third person and that time there would have been no one between both of us. I could easily put my queries in front of Him without hesitation.

You must be thinking to narrate this story to your friends, relatives, etc. By making it more interesting because it is very easy to narrate, just like a fairytale but more difficult and painful to experience it with courage and that courage I was given by Allah. Otherwise it would not have been easy for me to live in a body, which couldn't move or do anything of one's wish. One can only desire but cannot turn that desire into gain.

□

19

A New Beginning

It had been almost one year since I was sitting idle at home. I would say it was very dull. During daytime, I had the feeling of not being able to do much in life. This could be seen from my face. My Bua Aisha noticed it and asked my mother that they should send me out and not keep me confined within the boundaries of the house or else I would go into depression.

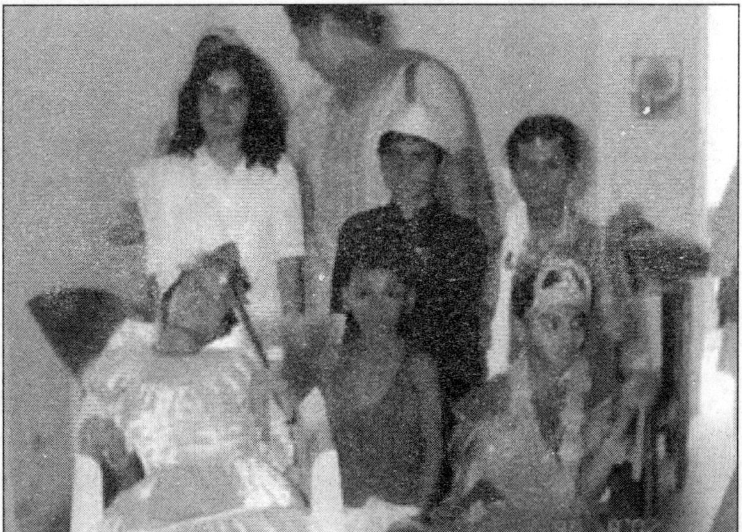

Zeenat seen as a fairy in her first school function in the year 2002.

So, my mother thought that she was right and went out in search of a good school, where I could comfortably interact with others as well as get a proper coaching. But, unfortunately, her search went in vain. She couldn't find any school of my suitability.

Then a few months later, somebody informed her about a special school named Shankara in Sector 33, Noida. Rizwana and Jamal, both my parents, took me to that school for admission.

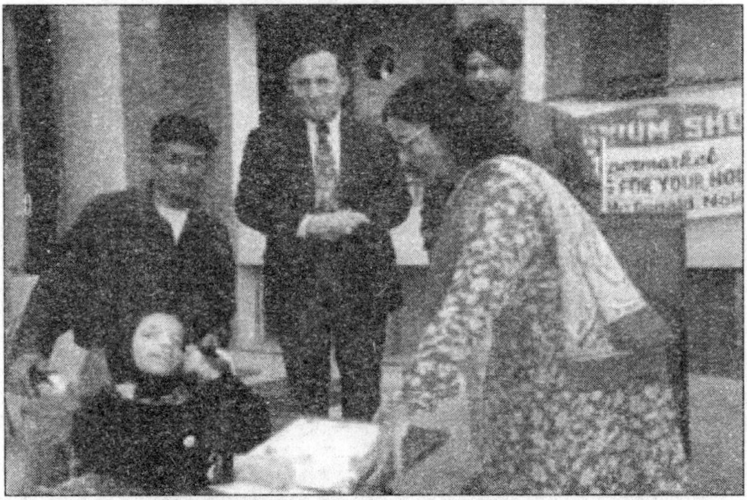

Zeenat receiving the first prize in a drawing competition organised by Khetan Public School in the year 2003.

Administration of that school was so poor that they made me lie down in the reception hall and the principal didn't even come to greet me, although she knew me well as I was very popular. I had received a letter from President Dr. A.P.J. Abdul Kalam for making his portrait and used to win first prizes whenever these schools held drawing competitions.

After treating me so badly, they forced my parents to get me admitted in their school.

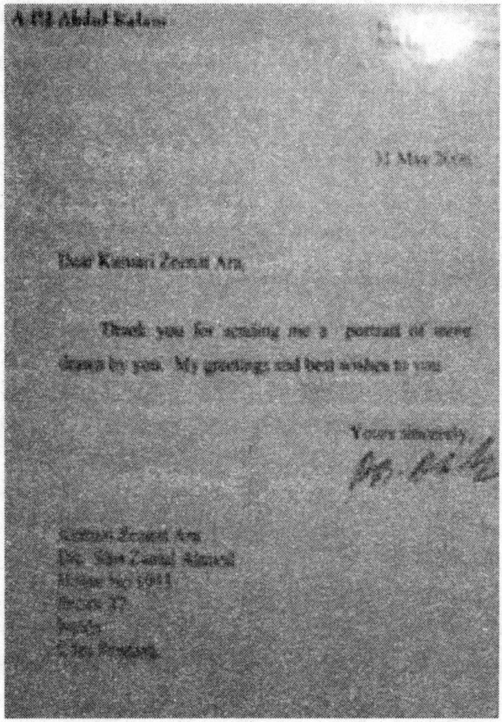
A P J Abdul Kalam

Dear Kumari Zeenat Ara,

Thank you for sending me a portrait of mine drawn by you. My greetings and best wishes to you.

Yours sincerely,

Zeenat received a letter from Dr. A.P.J. Abdul Kalam, former President of India, for making his portrait in May 2006.

Once they came back home from school, I said to them I wouldn't join that school as I was not satisfied with the way they turned out with me and then I decided I would study at home. For that I needed a tuition. So, I called Mrs. Negi Ma'am and explained my problem to her. After listening that, she suggested me to join a school in which she was already doing a job. She told me that the school was going to shift in a big area and was going to be one of the best schools of that city (Noida) where I was living.

Soon I was preparing to join that school. This time I was expecting to have the best guidance like that of a normal school.

□

20

Zeenat at MBCN School

This was the school Mrs. Negi Ma'am had told me about on phone. I went there with my parents for the admission. I felt very happy inside to find Mrs. Negi Ma'am there as well. Now she had become the vice principal of this school.

This school's name was Mata Bhagwanti Chadha Niketan. Mr. Ponty Sir was the owner of this school. I really salute him for his great work that he had started a school for children with special needs and pray for him that his soul stay in peace hereafter.

Whenever I think of him now, my eyes get filled with tears. He was a very nice person. I remember when I met him for the first time during the opening of the school, he told me, "Beta, if your interest is in fashion designing, don't take tension, just concentrate on your studies, as now you are in class 8th and leave that designing to me. I'll open a fashion house for you once you get over with your studies." He was also one of the greatest persons I have ever met and in just one meeting, he made a respectable image in my heart.

After the opening of school, perhaps I met him twice or thrice, I saw him spending his precious time with each child by visiting the classes, discussing their problems and comforting them personally. He never kept himself dependent on teachers or other authorities. He would talk to the children personally.

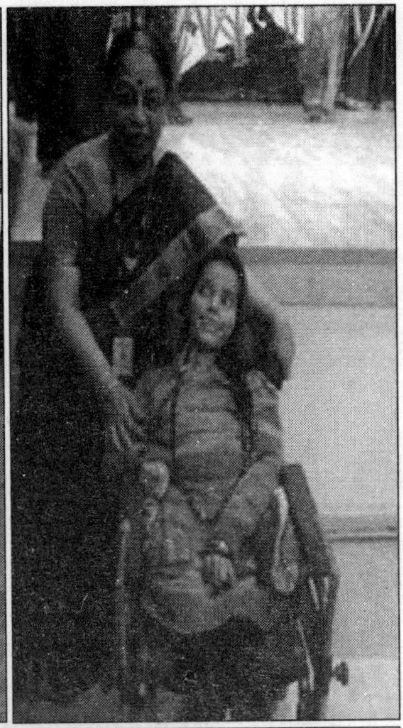

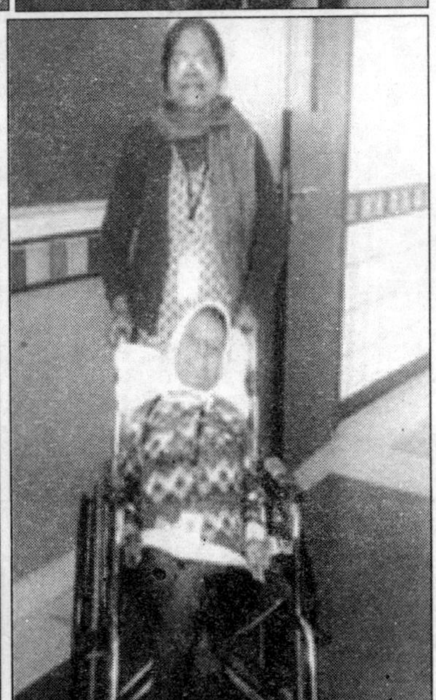

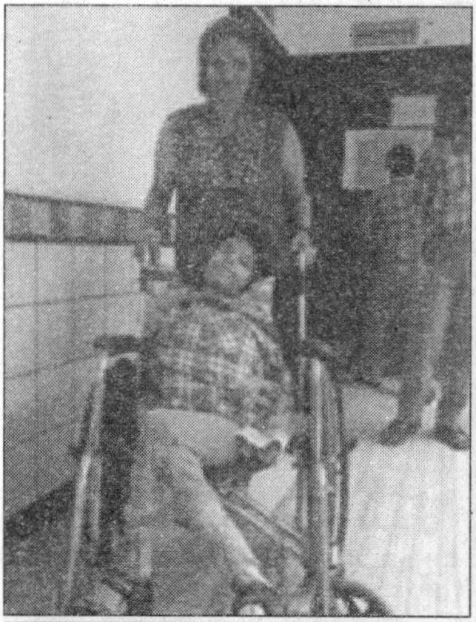

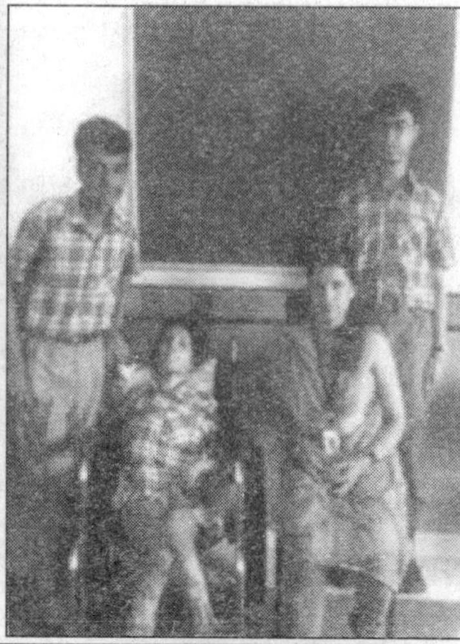

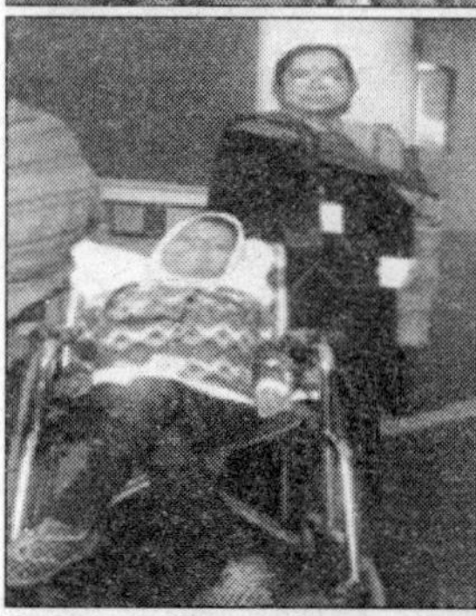

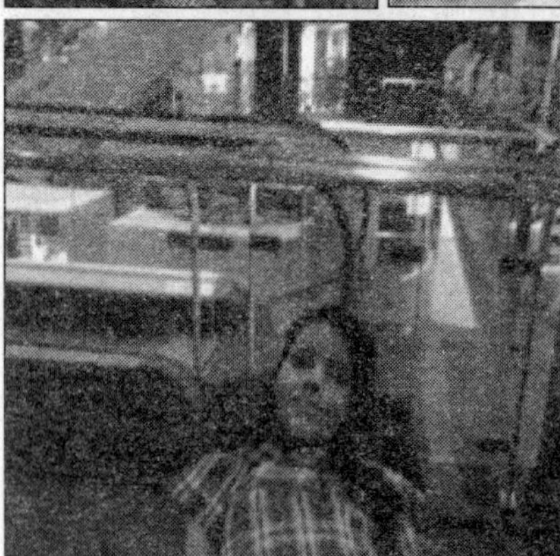

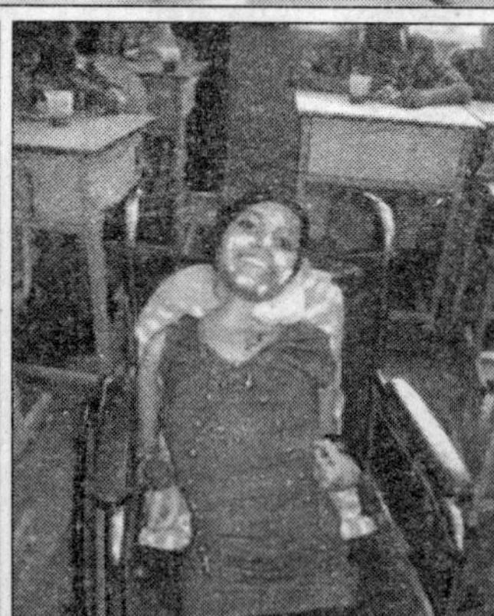

Zeenat with chief guest John Abraham in the annual day function at MBCN.

Memories of MBCN

When I went to that school for the first time after my admission, a new problem came in my life. It was that I had to go to the bus stop which was very far from my house, and secondly, my house was at the second floor. I needed someone's help who could bring me down the stairs and then take me to the bus stop regularly. Unfortunately, no one in my home had the time for that because my brother was in Aligarh at that time for his studies and my father did not stay at home full time and it was not possible for the females present at home to bring me down from the second floor. So I was very tense how I would join the school. It was to my luck that the problem got solved.

One of our neighbours, Shameem Aunty advised my mother to fix a rickshaw that could bring me down the stairs as well as take me to the bus stop.

My mother heeded the advice. She used to sit in the rickshaw and ask the rickshaw-puller or any other maid present at home to bring me down the floor. In this way, she would take me in her lap and go to the bus stop.

Although I didn't like that after a particular age a person take hold of me for bringing me down the stairs, but when you are in a such a problem, you become helpless. You have to surrender to the situation. It was what happened with me. I had to surrender at different levels of my life with big courage.

When my problem of reaching the bus stop had been solved, another cropped up. This time the problem was how I could sit in the bus when there was little balance in my body. But I am really very thankful to all teachers and attendants, who agreed to hold me in the bus. Their names were Bhawna Ma'am, Nirmal Ma'am, Chandana Gupta Ma'am, Mamta Ma'am, Rosy Ma'am. Jiya aunty and Suneeta Aunty both were attendants. They used to lie me down in the back seat of the bus and then put my head into their laps. In this way, I could easily reach the school.

When I reached the MBCN on the first day, I didn't require much adjustment as almost all staff, including the principal, Mrs. Vandana Sharma herself knew me well as I had been very popular among all teachers and schools due to my loving nature and, most importantly, my positive attitude towards all aspects of life. They generally knew me as we happened to meet in drawing competitions and debates held by different schools. So, there didn't arise much need of adjustment. I easily adjusted myself in that new school.

By the time in 2008 I joined that school, I was 21 years old. So, the principal Mrs. Vandana Ma'am promoted me directly from class 6th to class 8th as my age was more and she knew that I would cover it up soon, but unfortunately, initially I faced the same problem here also. There were no teachers who could guide me in all the subjects, but here I had a hope that things might become better and I would get a good opportunity as compared to the previous school.

Within two-three months of my joining, my problem had been solved. A new teacher came. Her name was Priya Nair Ma'am. She was a volunteer and especially put to teach me. She took the responsibility of the main subjects: Maths, Science and English.

I was very happy as her method of teaching was somewhat like that of Mrs. Negi Ma'am, and so I loved being taught by her.

□

21

After Joining MBCN I Started Enjoying Life More Than Before

When I was enrolled in this new school, I came to know that life is not that tough it had been with me. Once I started going to this school, life became easier for me. I got to know that life is very beautiful to live because we get it only once and the ultimate truth is death. So, I thought why we should waste it just crying over our woes all the time when the ultimate truth is death.

So, now you should know what change this school brought in my life. I am taking you back when I was 11 to 12 years old.

It was a time when all my three siblings used to go to school except Saif. In the weekend, two of my cousins, Taj and Attaullah used to visit us. If a new movie was released during that period, they took my siblings to watch it. They wouldn't take me due to the lack of facilities and another thing was that they would think how I could watch the movie among so many people, I could have fallen and got hurt.

But I would get hurt more from within, when they would take other three and leave me behind. I can't explain how bad I used to feel. Everyone would see my smiling face but nobody would see the pain in my eyes, a disappointment of not being able to see movies in a theatre.

But I am very thankful to my God (Allah, my designer) Who always showed this world that He never does prejudice with His humans. The same thing happened when I joined this school. God made watching movies so easy for me in the hall. Actually, the Centre Stage Mall was owned by Mr. Ponty Chadha, my school owner. That's why, our school used to take all students to watch movies in the hall twice a year. They would provide all comfort to children as they watched the movie in the hall.

When I saw a movie for the first time in the hall with my schoolmates, it was a very different experience for me. It was like dream come TRUE. God made this school a source of fulfilling my dreams.

After that, I saw many more movies in the hall. I can't remember the count. I would go to watch the movie with my siblings also in the same hall. The attendant over there would help me a lot when I would tell them that I have come from the MBCN School.

□

22

I Got Two New Friends in MBCN

As I have told you, this school brought many changes in my life. It also made me meet many nice people, and they included Nishchal and Kritika.

They made my life more meaningful. I learnt so many things from Kritika. You must have remembered I told you about Ranjana, my first friend whom I met in my first school. I missed her presence in this new school. I thought if she would have been there with me, I could have enjoyed still more, but when I met Kritika, I found her more interesting and learnt so many new things to improve my life, which was not so in Ranjana's case.

Actually, Kritika did her schooling from a normal school. She joined this school as a volunteer. She also had a problem in her lower limbs. Whenever I get tired of one-hour-long class, I would go to medical room to take some rest. She would also come with me. We would talk for long. I could share everything with her. There were three people in my life with whom I can openly share my feelings. They were Erum (my sister), Kritika and Ranjana.

Whenever I would share my pain with her, I felt good. It felt like half of my pain was over. She always encouraged me, "Zeenat, you have capabilities to achieve more in life, maybe more than me. So, please never lower down your morale." I always followed this line but one thing my heart never agreed upon when I used to say to her, "Why didn't you go for higher studies to become a doctor or engineer?" At this, she would say, "It's not very easy, yaar (friend) because people are not that supportive in schools and colleges. They misbehave with the disabled. I have joined the special school because here people understand the disable's needs and are very supportive as well."

Maybe she was right because she did her schooling with normal children. But truly believe me, my heart never agreed upon it, because my belief was that nobody could stop you from achieving anything until the supreme power wills.

Now you should know about Nishchal. He had a visual problem. He was studying in the same class as I was. He joined this school after five months of my joining.

He happened to be very helpful. In the class, although teachers were very helpful, yet sometimes they got busy in teaching other students and then if I would need to bring out my books from the bag, I usually didn't want to disturb them, and so Nishchal would bring out my books. I never asked of him, but he himself came to my help. He helped not only me, but also others if they were physically weak.

So, every time my problem would get solved before I actually faced it. Allah always brought me the succour.

□

23

Mrs. Priya Left the School

It was the time when Mrs. Priya Ma'am was teaching me and things were going as per my wish. Now I was very happy and felt that my classes would be completed peacefully since Mrs. Priya Ma'am was teaching me with full dedication. That was my best time I did ever spend during any teacher's classes, more relaxed, no tension about the doubts I might have encountered during the classes. However, this happiness didn't last longer. Mrs. Priya Ma'am also left the school in almost one year of her stay. She was a very nice teacher. I missed her presence all the time being at school.

The moment I knew about this news, all my dreams stood shattered. Mrs. Priya Ma'am herself told me this with a heavy voice. At this I controlled my emotions and tried hard to make her stay calm because I knew how much she had been attached to all children at school. So, I forgot about myself and went ahead to lessen her pain.

Mrs. Priya Ma'am left that school in just 20 days before the school's summer break after providing children with the final results. I had also given final exams but my entire syllabus was not fully completed at the end of the session. So, I was not promoted to class 9th by her because she wanted me to complete the remaining course in order I could be in a position to do much better in class 9th.

□

24

Again the Problem of Good Guidance Faced by Me

After a long two months' break, the school reopened. In the normal course, it generally becomes a big burden for the school-going students to attend school again after a long break, but it was not so in my case. It was like a new life for me. I would get a chance to interact with new people, I would have been able to know others' points of view for the same things. Going to school was just like I am in another world.

You can imagine my feelings here if you put yourself in my place. Just imagine how life would be like if it is confined within the boundaries of your body and you can't move an inch by your own wish even if your back is aching and you cannot turn it to get some relief.

That was why I wanted to go to school as much as possible because then I could keep my body in motion, but due to frequent illness, I would not have been able to do that.

When I went to school after vacation, I came to know about the plan to promote me to class 10thwhen I hadn't even fully completed class 8th due to my frequent illness and another thing there was no proper guidance for even a particular subject. When they asked me for anything, I agreed to it since I was getting older with everyday, and so I wanted to complete class 12th as soon as possible in order to do some professional course, so that I could be an independent girl in the future.

Now the time came to select the subjects. Everyone at school suggested me not to take science because it requires lots of hard work and it might hamper my health as I was very weak and got ill very often, but I wanted something else. I had interest in science. So, I didn't consider their suggestion and went back home and asked my younger sister Erum, who had completed class 12th by that time.

My sister advised me to go for science since in class 10th, it teaches basics and so it is very important for all of us. Actually, the board from which I was doing my class 10th would have been providing choices for subjects in class 10th as well.

After selection of subjects, my cousin Taj Bhai went to the NIOS Institute and got me registered there. He used to go to the institute whenever I needed.

I started studying myself because till then, there was no proper guidance at school, although principal, Mrs. Vandana promised me to make it available soon.

Zeenat celebrating her birthday with her sister Erum Fatima at MBCN School in 2008.

□

25

The Person Who Loved Me most Diagnosed with Tumour

My Bua, Aisha, with whom I had been since my birth, who used to sleep next to me, who got me ready for the school because my mother would have been busy with other children all the time, was not going well. She was having pain in her abdomen and her stomach got enlarged due to tumour.

Earlier, she was diagnosed with swelling in her abdomen. Later, in a proper medical examination, everybody got to know about this horrifying disease. My parents didn't tell her about this because then it might have become difficult for her to live the remaining life peacefully. The doctors had already told my father that her tumour could not be operated at the age she was. She was above 70.

Nobody at home told me as well about this because they knew how much I had been attached to her. She was just like my own real biological mother. Sometimes, when I would have had severe pain in my legs, especially at nights, my Bua, Aisha would apply oil all over my legs and press them hard till the time I got relief. She would make herself awake all night if I needed her help. That was her love for me. She loved me maybe as she loved my mother.

But soon I came to know about her problem when my younger sister, Erum took her again for a medical examination. The doctor informed that her tumour was becoming larger very rapidly. On hearing this, my sister couldn't control her emotions and kept crying throughout the way without Bua letting know about this.

When she reached home, there were still tears in her eyes. She straightaway ran into the room in which I was lying down. She embraced me. Then both of us cried hard long. In her broken voice, she told me everything. When I listened to her carefully, it made me numb. I feared and shivered because I had already faced the impact of this disease before when my elder brother was suffering from it.

I sobbed a while and then thought what my life would be like in the absence of my Bua. Suddenly, the same thing flashed off in front of my retina. I closed my eyes instantly with the fear as if my temperature was going down from normal and the body became too cool in that hot month of July.

After some time, I became normal when my sister told me that the doctor had said that Bua would be all right soon with the medicine going.

□

26

Preparation for Class 10th was the Top Priority

After having lived with such a big disease, my Bua never went to take rest. She always preferred to help my mother as much as she could have been able to do in daily household work. She would make me get ready for school even when she was not feeling well.

I myself loved her a lot that whenever I would think of her disease, I would ask God to make me independent or provide me with strength to walk, so that I could also do something for my Bua, who spent all her life in upbringing me well.

During the period of her illness, when she used to send me to school, I would think of her throughout the way to school. I would murmur some blessings and prayed to Allah to bring her into a well-being state, but once I reached the school, one more thought would take place in my mind – it was to complete class 10th as soon as possible and so I would struggle for that.

In my school, there were ramps in all areas of necessities for easy access by the students. So, my attendant Suneeta Aunty would pick me from the parking lot of the school and take me into a wheelchair to the classroom, but before going to class, I used to ask her to take me to the principal's office and with her help, I visited the principal's office more often with the demand of providing a science and economics teacher.

Principal Vandana Ma'am always considered my queries but the problem was that the number of students for these particular subjects was few or, you can say, there were none. All the students had arts subjects. Hence, it was not possible for the principal to hire a teacher for a particular student because she had to answer further.

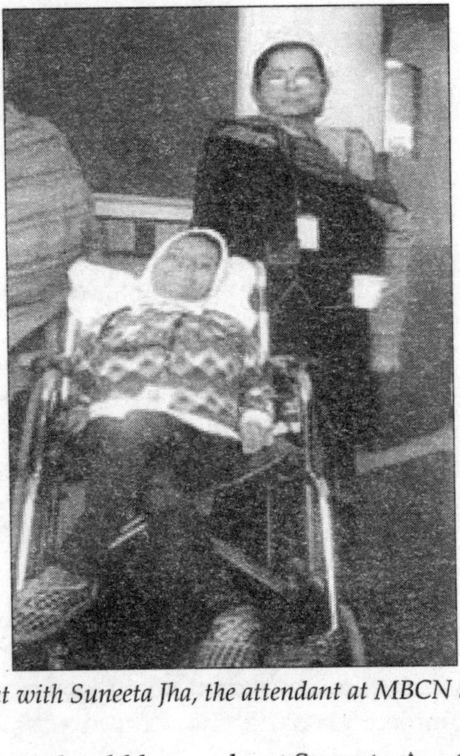

Zeenat with Suneeta Jha, the attendant at MBCN School.

Now you should know about Suneeta Aunty, who also played a significant role in my life.

Suneeta Aunty was amongst the very few female attendants or, you can say, only one who knew well how to keep me sit properly in a wheelchair with more comfort and due to this expertise, she was kept to look after me at school by Vandana Ma'am.

She used to feed me in lunch time and as I had a little problem in swallowing, I rarely ate solids. I used to eat semi-solid, but sometimes, in my school canteen, when I found out that Wilson Bhaiya had prepared Sāmbhar Dosa, I would ask Aunty to feed me the same. At this, she would bring it for me from the canteen, smash it and then feed me. It was her own skill to feed me all types of solid food according to my comfort.

□

27
Big News

My Bua, Aisha was always worried about me and would think over it more often. She would think what would happen to me after her and my parents, who would look after me, as I was totally dependent on others for even a small thing. I would require others' help for all my necessities. I couldn't do anything of my own. So, many a time, when she would sit along with all family members, she would demand of my father and mother to do something. She would say, "I want her to be secure before my death."

And obviously in her point of view, she was right. Anybody who had been in her place must have said the same. Her worry for me was justified. A girl who is dependent on others for all her requirements, who can't put her need in front of others or ask for it very easily, she will hesitate somewhere in her heart because she doesn't have control on others except on her own self. That was the big reason why my Bua wanted me to be secure before her death.

But I never had that feeling. I believed if Allah had sent me with this problem. There must be some reason behind it. He must have some plan for me.

And it was true. Allah never let my wishes go waste, as well as never let my smile fly off my face. It was maintained till the time of my birth.

One day I was lying down on the bed watching TV, my mother was also present there. She asked me, "With whom will you stay: Erum or Mazhar?" Suddenly I answered, "Mummy, I will stay in my own house." It was like Allah had made me utter these words out of my mouth, and the same day in the evening, my family got news that in Noida, they had won a plot in my name.

They got to know about this news when one of our neighbours, Mr. Mushtaq Uncle, who had been my father's friend also, living a little far away from my home, called on my father's number and let him know that he had won a plot in my name in Noida authority. At this, my father enquired how come he was so sure. His neighbour told him that he also had given his name in that draw but didn't win it as his son (Shadab Bhai) was checking it on the internet. Only Zeenat's name was showing.

My father was so happy. He never expected that someday that thing would ever happen to them because he had already tried that in all family members' names in many draws released by the Noida authority but such big news they had never received.

The draw in which they had given my name was cancelled four years earlier and the money was given back to my father. Only a small amount was left with the authority. So, they had almost forgotten about it.

But as I told you, Allah never rejects words spoken out of my mouth. So, he might be listening to me when I said to my mother that I would live in my own house.

□

28

A Tragedy that Almost Broke Me Dawn

My Bua, with whom I was so attached, maybe the most in my family, was not behaving the same as she used to. I had been observing some changes in her behaviour since 2-3 months after Erum took her for a medical checkup.

I felt that my Bua had started maintaining a distance from me. She would sleep down the floor next to my bed and when I would ask her the reason behind this, she would say, "Now you are a grown up girl. You should learn to sleep alone." The distance which my Bua kept from me was Allah's order because if it had not been done, it would have been difficult for me to live apart from her. Allah automatically put that thought about maintaining a distance into her mind. God can do anything if He wants to, and He is the creator as well as the only controller of this world.

Days passed by and so my Bua's condition deteriorated day by day. So, she herself asked my father to send her to her native place. She had all her relatives over there and wanted to meet them.

My father sent her at once. Both my parents didn't want to send her to the native place because she was not going well and here in Noida, we could have provided her with a better treatment, but being an obedient brother, he never said 'no' to her. She reached her native place comfortably and then within one week, she left this world. I was unaware about that truth for one month because nobody at home told me. But I was not a kid, who could not read others' faces. I was a mature girl and when I got to know about that truth, it hurt me immensely. I kept crying all the time, about which my siblings didn't know. They told me my Bua would come soon as her treatment was going there and Ammi and Abbu had gone to see her.

When my parents came back from my native place's after the burial of my Bua, they didn't know that I kept crying more often without letting them know that I knew the truth.

I thought if they didn't want to tell me, then let it be as it was. If I had told them that I knew the truth, I wouldn't get my Bua back.

Now after my Bua's death, I would sleep either with my sister Erum or with my mother. I went through the times when I needed somebody's help to change my posture while sleeping as body starts aching if you are in the same posture for a long time.

Actually, when my Bua was alive, she used to change my position throughout the night and, after her death, whenever I needed help to change my position at night, I generally wouldn't disturb the person sleeping next to me because when I expected to take help from them, I would find them in a good sleep, and then I would try hard to change my posture myself. When I was not able to do that, tears would start streaming down my eyes as the part of my body which I wanted to move wouldn't even go ahead a single inch after long efforts and then it would be paining a lot.

With eyes full of tears, I would mumble, "Allah, why have you done this to me? At least, you could have given me that much of strength so that I could move my body parts." The very moment I would speak out these words, somebody would come out from their bed for their own need and then I would call him or her for help.

Allah would always listen to my words just before a single tear floated down my cheeks. That is why, I always say that if Allah has sent me with this problem, He must have sent found solution for that as well.

□

29

Problems Faced by Me After My Bua's Death

I have already told you that after my Bua left this world, I faced many problems at night because when she was alive, she used to take very good care of me during night hours.

She was present all the time when I needed her. If I wanted to turn my head, she woke up at my one voice. In her presence, I could sleep comfortably.

What she did for me may be sometimes difficult even for a mother to do that for her own children. She sacrificed all her life in giving me proper care. Till her last breath, she had the belief that someday I would start walking by my own. For that, she applied many Unani oils on my whole body religiously everyday, and used to give me homeopathic medicine, but nothing worked.

Although her effort went in vain, she didn't lose hope. She had big dreams for me. She used to say, "I want to see my Bettiya in red veil. I will have my life's big day when my Bettiya will become a bride."

I remember, one month before her death, she told everyone at home, "Please, you all never say anything to my bitiya. Even in case something wrong has been done by her, always keep her happy." And then she started crying.

She was my big support because I found her around me all the time, you can say that she was in my service for 24 hours with devotion. You can purchase service with money but devotion can come only with love. Its price is love, which is not very easy to earn. I was lucky that I had it. My Bua loved me a lot. She devoted all her life upbringing me.

After her death, my Mom's life became more hectic because now she had to manage both kitchen as well as me alone. My father was busy all the time in his professional life. He never had time to contribute to my mother in sending me to school or making me sleep comfortably at night, so that my mother got some relief at least at night. He found himself very busy all the time.

Allah has solutions for all problems. In those times, one of my cousins, Farhan, who was doing his engineering from Greater Noida, would come to my house in the weekend. He had the habit to sleep late at night. My Mummy used to tell him, "Beta Gufraan, please look after Manni till you are awake."

'Gufraan' was his pet name. And he looked after me very well in all weekends. He also listened to me in one call. My sister Erum also felt very relieved when he was at home because I started sleeping next to her after one year of my Bua's death.

She was also very understanding. She told my Mom, "You sleep in another room, I will make Manni sleep next to me. You just don't worry. You have to manage household work in day hours. You need to take rest at night."

It was very difficult to live life for me after Bua's death because I received her service before I actually needed it.

She got to know what I needed before I actually I felt its requirement. So, after her death, I couldn't expect the same from others. There had been a limit of help I could have asked for from others. I couldn't take help from others at night more often, because they have their own life also.

They have to go to college or office, etc. in the morning. In that case, I couldn't disturb others any time. They also needed rest for some time.

Sometimes, I would feel very helpless and pray to Allah, "Why have you created my life so full of limitations. I also have a soul. I also feel pain like others." Then automatically after some time, I would feel relieved and get ready to face the challenges coming my way.

What I used to do then was that I would sleep in a posture in which I could sleep for long hours. And you can't believe my body ache lessened greatly as compared to what it used to be when my Bua was alive. Sometimes, I could sleep alone. Allah had made things easier for me.

□

30

A New Volunteer Agreed to Teach Me Science

As my principal, Mrs. Vandana had promised me to make available a teacher for science and economics, she was trying her best in order to fulfil her promise. She even contacted a few coaching centres asking them if she could send me to their coaching centres during school hours, but they said they didn't take school students in the morning hours. They took them in the evening classes because they had morning time reserved for the engineering students.

Zeenat Ara with her principal, Mrs. Vandana Sharma at MBCN School.

When she shared this

problem with me, I kept patience and left everything to Allah (God) and went ahead, studied whatever I could myself. Then, in a few days, I got news that one volunteer used to come twice a week and she would teach me both the subjects. Her name was Mrs. Sangeeta. I was very happy and thanked Allah.

Mrs. Sangeeta was also a very nice teacher. She taught me very well, although, in those periods, I was not going well. I had weakness due to which I got ill more often and so I rarely attended school. Many of my classes was generally missed.

□

31

The Biggest Challenge of My Life

Time was passing very rapidly and so my challenges were also increasing day by day. This was the time, say in or around 2010, when I was at the end of my adolescence period and was on the threshold of my adulthood. I was now a fully mature girl.

I knew well what was good for me and what was bad. The biggest challenge came in my life during this period because being a young girl, I didn't like to be helped by any other person. In case I wanted to move somewhere, I didn't like people carry me in their arms while changing my place. It was all very embarrassing for me. I really didn't like all this, but I was helpless I could not do anything into it since I couldn't move of my own due to my suffering from SMA disease.

And it was a normal feeling. Any girl would have felt the same if she would have been in my place. I can't explain to you that situation in words how difficult it had been for me, but since, in spite of all these limitations, I couldn't keep my world confined within four walls of my room, I would have to fight bravely this challenge also, and I did that. Here you can't live my pain. You can only feel it in your imagination.

I would feel very embarrassed when in need I was being carried by any other male person. Suppose, in case I needed to go to school or in another case where I had to go out of my house, I would require someone's help as at that time, my brother was in Aligarh for his studies.

If he were at home, I would feel comfortable because both my sister and brother would never say no to me. Both of them used to take me anywhere I wished to. I took my sister along to school if I needed her but they never got irritated. If at night my brother was not much tired and he felt even a slight hint that I was asking for help, he would come immediately and make me comfortable. Like earlier I have told you that at night, I needed to change my position as my back started aching. He would come and make me feel comfortable by changing my position but, unfortunately, now my brother was away from home.

I got myself stuck in a situation in which I couldn't either blame the person who was supposed to help me or Allah (God) who put me in that situation. I had a firm faith in Allah and knew He would definitely bring me out of that situation soon.

I never had a problem with the person who used to help me to move me from one place to another. Rather I respect them because they would carry me very carefully, in a way such that I didn't get hurt. The problem was that I would feel very uncomfortable since I was not a baby or small girl then.

It is true that you can't feel my pain with the written description or spoken words until you don't put yourself in that situation. I was not left with any other option but to surrender to the situation.

□

32

Mrs. Sangeeta Took Back Step

Back at school, my preparation for board exams was going well for all subjects till that time when suddenly, Mrs. Sangeeta Ma'am told me that she wouldn't be able to teach me science further because she had got a job in the JP company. In spite of this, she assured me she would take out time and give me classes in economics.

Initially, when she told me that, I felt very bad and helpless but later on, after a few days, I held up myself. I was feeling helpless because very little time was left for my board exams and besides this, that little time would have become less because I would get ill very frequently.

Now with that small period of time, I had to find out a teacher as well as get myself prepared for the exams.

Mrs. Sangeeta Ma'am was a very good teacher and by profession, she was an architect. She taught me so well and according to my comfort that it became very difficult for me to find a teacher of that level.

You must know what type of comfort she had been providing me. Very few students get such a big honour by their teachers. She used to feed me during classes in case I didn't feel low. She would give me one bite after a small explanation.

□

33

Zeenat Read About Her Problem on the Net

Now I was 23 years old in the year 2011 and started having chest congestion very frequently, which resulted in my weakness as well as loss of my activities. My daily schedule would get disturbed. I would not have been able to attend school regularly. That problem I never used to have before. Only after one year-and-a-half later, I started having that frequent tightening in my chest.

When I became irritated of this problem, I decided to find out the reason behind this. I thought long, instantly a thought came in my mind and then I asked my father, "What problem had I been diagnosed with at my birth?" He told me that I had SMA type 2.

The very moment I got to know this, I went straight, searched it out on the Google. I found out that in SMA, children get their muscles weak and with the passage of time, it affects the entire body muscles. Once the weakness increases over time, its effect reaches lungs, leading to its congestion, due to which children start getting difficulty in breathing, congestion, tightening of chest, etc.

SMA is caused by a gene called SMN1, which is abnormal or missing in people with the disease. SMA is inherited in an autosomal recessive pattern, meaning that a child must inherit two copies of the defective gene, one from each parent. About 1 in 40 people carry a defective

SMN1 gene that they could pass on to their children. SMA affects both males and females of all ethnic backgrounds.

There are five or six types of SMA but I was suffering with type 2. Children with SMA are found to be very intelligent. The brain is not affected, and they have been tested to have at least average to above average intelligence.

Signs and Symptoms

The symptoms vary greatly depending on the SMA type involved, the stage of the disease, and individual factors. They commonly include:

- Overall muscle weakness, poor muscle tone.
- Difficulty in achieving developmental milestones, difficulty in sitting/standing/walking.
- In infants: adopting of a frog-leg position when sitting (hips abducted and knees flexed)
- Loss of strength of the respiratory muscles – weak cough, weak cry (infants), accumulation of secretions in the lungs or throat, respiratory distress.
- Bell-shaped torso.
- Clenched fists with sweaty hands.
- Head often tilted to one side, even when lying down.
- Fasciculation (twitching) of the tongue.
- Difficulty sucking or swallowing, poor feeding.
- Weight lower than normal.

Treatment

There is no known cure for spinal muscular atrophy till date. But research going in stem cell therapy shows a big hope for patients with SMA.

Palliative Care Includes the Following:

- **Orthopaedics:** Weak spine muscles may lead to development of kyphosis; scoliosis and other orthopaedic problems. So, a patient should be kept under the observation of a physiotherapist and an occupational therapist to avoid such complications.

- **Respiratory Care:** The respiratory system requires utmost attention in SMA as once weakened, it never fully recovers. Impaired cough reflex poses a constant risk of respiratory infection and pneumonia. The patient must consult doctors as soon as possible at the time of illness.
- **Nutritional Care:** Difficulties in jaw opening, chewing and swallowing food might have made it difficult for the patients to have adequate amount of nutrition. So, it is advisable for a patient to eat more frequently than healthy people to avoid reduction of muscles.
- **Mobility:** Assistive technologies may help in managing movement and daily activity and greatly increase the quality of life.

Onset of SMA Type 2:

Children are diagnosed before 2 years of age, usually about 15 months of age. These children are usually able to be in a sitting position without support in their early age, but often cannot get there by themselves. They can sometimes crawl with bracing and therapy, and on occasion, may stand with braces but it wasn't so in my case. Feeding and swallowing problems are not common in Type 2 children, though they are still possible. They will usually never walk. The lifespan of a Type 2 child varies so widely. There isn't one! They could pass away at an early age or they could live well into adulthood. As with all forms of SMA, weakness increases over time.

At the end of the discovery, I became a little nervous, but I didn't lose hope. I knew any problem or big huddle that would come in my way could not break my will-power or make me weak since God was always there to help me and He would give me strength to fight with that deadly disease.

□

34

Search Continued for Science Teacher

I was becoming very depressed since it was just a few days back that I had got to know what exactly the problem I had been suffering from and besides this, I was worried about a science teacher.

When I went to school, there was a piece of news that a science teacher had been appointed for me, on listening that I was very happy and excited to meet her.

The next day when I met her, I didn't find her teaching that good as that of Mrs. Sangeeta Ma'am. She was teaching so-so, not good, not bad, and in Mrs. Sangeeta Ma'am's case, obviously she was an architect, so there must have been no comparison between them.

That new teacher, Gunjan Ma'am taught me for three months and left my syllabus in the middle because she was pregnant and left school on leave for the time being. When I went back home, I decided to take home tuition or else my syllabus wouldn't be complete in time. Moreover, I would require extra time to prepare it as I got ill often.

As soon as this thing came in my mind, I directly called on Mrs. Priya Ma'am's number and asked her if she could give me home tuition. At once she didn't confirm it, instead she said, "Let me first visit you and check your syllabus, then only I will take any step ahead."

The day she visited my place, she found me very happy because my search for science teacher seemed to be over.

Who could have taught me better than her? She was a very qualified teacher.

Once she went through my entire syllabus, she was satisfied. She knew she could teach me, but again a problem came. It was the distance between my home and her home. She told me she might not be able to come regularly. So, it would be better for me to talk to somebody else. For that, she had given me the number of a teacher.

□

35
Home Tuition Seemed to Turn Out Good

I called on the number given by Priya Ma'am. The person who received the call was Mr. Balwant. He used to run a coaching centre. I told him everything regarding myself, my problem, the way I used to study, etc. and asked him if he could teach me even then. He told me yes, and came the day after in the evening. I showed him all my syllabus. He told me he would be taking my classes from the next day. I agreed to it, but somewhere in my heart, I felt that he wouldn't be able to teach me because his voice was not clear. He stammered a lot.

Next day in the afternoon, he called on my number and told me that he wouldn't be able to come on days I wanted him to be there since he took engineering students on those days and a new teacher would take over my classes.

The same day in the evening, the new teacher called on me. The moment I heard his voice, I kept quiet for a while, then I felt relaxed. I was satisfied at least he did not stammer like the previous teacher. He let me know that he would be taking my classes on the days best suited to me. I was very happy because I was going to have classes as per my schedule.

As I keep on telling you I have firm belief in God, that no power exists as Him and He can change things within no time if He wants to, the same way Allah might have listened to my prayers and sent me a good teacher in the form of an angel to teach me. Do you know Allah sends angels to those with whom he is pleased?

When he came for the trial class, my mother gave him all the information regarding me and asked about him as well. He told her that he was a B. Tech 3rd year student from AMITY UNIVERSITY, NOIDA. He was doing his B. Tech in mechanical engineering.

When my mother brought him inside to introduce me, I asked him, "Sir, have a seat please." His name was Sameer, which was intact in my mind since the day I met him. Actually I was fond of this name from Salman Khan's movies. He usually kept this name in his movies.

He sat just next to the bed I was lying down on. People generally would have been confused how to teach me, since lying down on the bed, I can't even hold the book, but this didn't seem from his face if he was facing any problem while teaching me. He was a very understanding and bighearted man. He would never let me feel that I was different from others in any aspect of life.

At the end of the class, I asked him, "Sir, you must have felt difficulty while reading my handwriting." He said, "Why, what is the problem with your handwriting? It is perfect. I can easily understand it. If you will see my handwriting, you will be faint. You know, it's really very poor."

In fact, his writing was excellent. It was as clear as a piece of diamond and seemed as if beads are spread all over the paper. Later, I got to know about it when I received an assignment given by him.

I asked him about my writing because teachers at school used to face difficulty in understanding my writing except Mrs. Negi Ma'am. So, I thought he too might have felt the same since he was so young as compared to other teachers and must have never seen any person like me ever in life. In this way, I wanted to clear out all my doubts in the beginning so that I wouldn't feel any difficulty later.

□

36

Teacher Received Very Bad Treatment in Return

Now my problem of science teacher seemed to be solved. Again Sameer Sir came to teach me. Every time he would find me ready for the class, because he had told me that I should be ready on time as he himself had to study for his course.

He was teaching me very well and would try all the possible ways to clear out my doubts. Still then my doubts remained.

I said to him, "Sir, I am not getting what you are teaching me." He said, "Until or unless you will not tell me your problem exactly, how will I solve it?"At this question I couldn't be able to answer him.

He would say, "If you are not able to see properly since you have been lying down on the bed, I will write in big letters. That's my problem. You should not worry about it." He always kept on asking me my problem but I would tell him, "Sir, I am not getting with the method you are teaching me." Initially, I thought he is not capable to teach and must not have done well in his studies.

But the problem was that he was teaching me from the guide because I hadn't received the study material till then. I got to know the problem later after my board exams.

Many a time, I would think my teacher was right. I might not be able to understand because I used to study lying down on the bed. So, to get over with that problem, I would ask my mother, "Mummy, please make me sit before sir comes." And when Sameer Sir would see me sitting, he would ask me, "Why did you trouble yourself when I can teach you according to your comfort. No need to punish yourself, just lie down on the bed, I'll teach you. I'll write big, you can understand that then."

He was a very nice person, though inexperienced, but much more than an experienced teacher. He had sympathy and a soft corner for me somewhere in his heart.

Later, I felt, whenever I would try to make him understand my limitations so that he wouldn't feel difficulty while teaching me, I would find him not paying attention to it. Rather he instantly switched over to some other topic. Maybe he didn't want to have me hurt again and again due to my physical problem.

He would come and go but my doubts remained from where they had started. I got irritated as well as irresistible because my exams were coming nearer with the days passing. I spoke out very bitter words to him. I said to him, "Sir, I am not getting with the way you are teaching me." Then he said, "What should I do then, there is no solution except I should stop teaching you and bring you some other substitute." At this, I kept quiet, then after some time I replied back, "I think you don't know how to teach. I have a better solution for you. Go to AMITY in asset department, the same department in which you are studying currently. There is a teacher named Mrs. Sangeeta. She taught me for some time. She will make you learn how to teach science." He smiled and said, "Yeah, sure, why not tell me her full name. I will definitely meet her. At least finally you reached a solution, big achievement for me."

Sangeeta Ma'am was the same volunteer who had taught me science and economics for a few months at school. As I told you, she was an architect. So, she used to give classes to architectural students at AMITY, NOIDA.

I always insulted him but he never minded it and took it lightly as if nothing had happened. Although after the class, I would feel guilty to have behaved with him like that because I happened to be a very obedient student with all my teachers and so I am never supposed to behave with him so rudely, but whatever I was doing with him was a spontaneous act over which I didn't have any control. I had become irritated since my board exams were drawing nearer, but till then, my syllabus wasn't fully completed.

One day, when he was teaching me, my cousin Farhan (my Mama's son), who came in the weekend, was sitting nearby and observing me throughout the class and after class, he found that he was teaching me excellently. He said, "Manni (Zeenat), you won't get any better teacher than him. He is teaching you from the basics, just make good use of it, don't confuse yourself."

Farhan, my cousin, always gave me the best advice. He was just like a real brother for me and wanted all my dreams to be fulfilled soon. For that, he himself would help me. Whatever he could. I too would respect him a lot. But, when he said that I should not let that teacher go. I didn't consider it much and next day, I called Sameer Sir and said, "Sir, send me a substitute today."

□

37

My Feeling of Regret

I was very upset because my problem of getting a proper teacher was not being solved despite putting a great effort. Everybody at home advised me that I should not be in a hurry in taking a decision since Sameer Sir was teaching well but I took my decision and called for the substitute.

The substitute came the very next day at the same time Sameer sir used to teach me. The moment he entered my room, he was confused and went out. An indecision of how to teach me was clearly visible on his face. And it is obvious for anyone to be confused if he or she has to teach someone whom he finds in a flat position. He didn't seem to decide the direction from which to proceed to teach; some of the sort was felt by him as I observed.

He started teaching me and when I couldn't learn it the way he taught, he shouted at me and said, "I will give you a slap." At that time, no one was there around me in the room. Only two of us were present there. I had a big shock. I never expected this from any of my teachers. In the meanwhile, I realised Sameer Sir's importance. How could anybody even shout or talk about slapping a person, who is already suffering?

I reverted to all positive traits of Sameer Sir. I recalled there were no such expressions on his face when he saw me first. Instead when I had said to him, "Sir, I just want to pass in this subject," he had said to me with a mild smile, "No,

I will make you score 90 percent marks and for that, you need not make changes to your position. I will teach you in a position you are comfortable with."

In case I faced difficulty to focus on the written matter, since I was lying down all the time, he would bring the notebook close to my eyes, hold it there and then teach me. By bending his back long, he must have had back pain but he would do so for me so that I could comfortably understand the written part.

Then, suddenly, I thought of the present situation and at the end of the class, I made up the mind that I would call back Sameer Sir and get tuition from him only. He is surely the best teacher for me.

Next day, when I called him again, he told me that he would come to teach me, but when he didn't come even after many days, I asked my mother to call him up. When my mother called him up, he told her that his training for three months was going to start. For that, he might go somewhere else. So, he wouldn't be able to give me a long time.

Actually, once before he had already put into my ears during our classes that he might leave teaching me any moment because he could have to go anywhere for the training.

Now I was at a point where I had started from. I had to find a new teacher again. I felt regret about what. I had done with Sameer Sir. Being a young student, he came out to be a very good teacher.

□

38

A New Teacher came at School

I was revising my lesson in the classroom when the HOD (Gupta Ma'am) came in and introduced me with a new teacher appointed for the science subject. Her name was Neelam. She had done her M.Sc. in maths and was a teacher in a normal school before joining the MBCN. She had joined there just because of her son Shittij.

She took my syllabus so fast that it had been completed in time, just one month before my exams were supposed to be held. She taught me not that good as I expected from her, considering her degree but she tried her best.

One thing I can't deny is that she did whatever she could do to clear out my doubts, although it was another thing that the subject she was teaching me was not her subject. She had done her masters in maths.

□

39

Zeenat Develops Interest in Dress Designing

I was good at sketching, I was drawing very well since the time I was 15 years old. I got a skill by which I could imagine a thing and then could turn that imagination into a sketch on a piece of paper. Everyone, whether far or close to me, would appreciate this quality of mine.

Handmade paintings by Zeenat.

But this quality couldn't stay longer with me since I was losing strength, which resulted in loss of hand movement. So, I would rarely take to drawing. Even then my passion in that area didn't diminish from my mind. I continued sketching in a small portion, like I stopped sketching

Paintings made by Zeenat on Computer.

scenery, desert, villages, cities, etc. Instead I developed interest in dress designing.

In dress designing, you need not draw much. You have to draw only the dress along with its colour scheme. It does not require much display of things around it like in a painting or drawing. It can be done on a small piece of paper also. So, it would have been easy for me to handle it.

So, one day when at school, my syllabus was already completed, and only revision was going on, my HOD (Gupta Ma'am) came into my classroom and informed me I had to create a lehngha collection for the next month because they were going to display my designs at the Centre Stage Mall, Noida, on the occasion of Disabled Day.

The CSM was owned by Mr. Ponty Chadha, my school owner. Because of that liberty, they had the right to organize any sort of function over there.

I was very happy when I heard about the opportunity because there was little I could have a chance to popularise my designs among more people. I had to speak a few lines on the biggest dream of my life in front of about 1,000 or more people.

I forgot about my exams for a while, and devoted myself into thinking of the lenhga designs as well as a good speech that could have stolen everyone's heart present there.

Display of Zeenat's designs at CSM Mall, Noida on Disabled Day.

The time had come and when my sister Erum called on my principal, Mrs. Vandana Ma'am's cabin to know about the exact time I had to reach the venue, she said, "Get Zeenat ready and apply a good make up on her. I want her look more beautiful." Although I didn't require much work on my face, Allah had already made me such that I was not in any need to apply external material to look beautiful. Allah knew she can't do things of her own. So, maybe he made things easier for me, enabling me to take less help from others. She enquired of my sister because she loved me a lot.

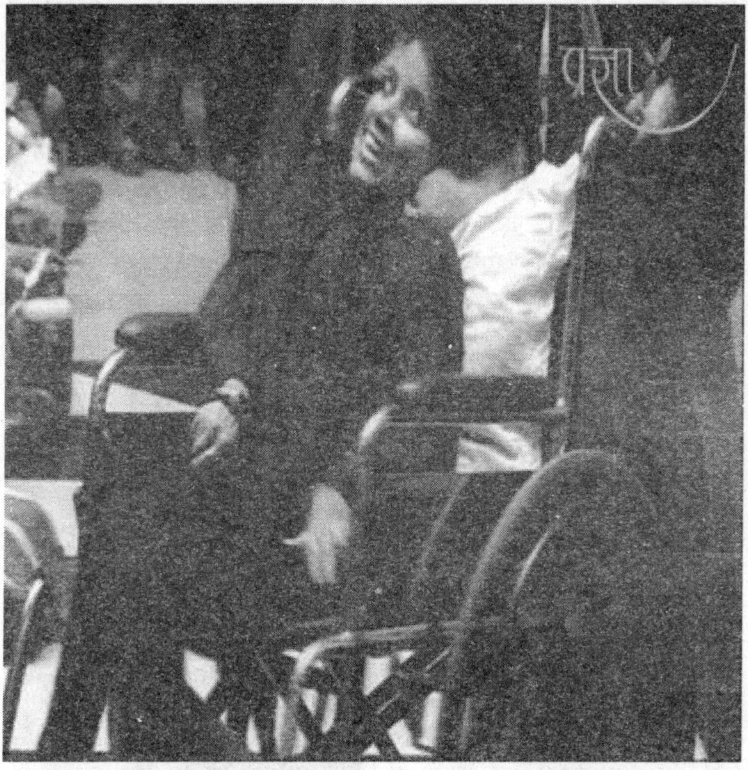

Zeenat Ara at CSM Mall, Sec. 18, Noida, celebrating Disabled Day.

I reached the venue on time. I was looking good. Even my principal didn't expect it. She said to me, "Zeenat, you are looking very fresh and beautiful." The anchor who was hosting the programme seemed to be fainting seeing me.

Soon after I got over with my speech, he came close to me and said, "Will you be my girlfriend?" And at once I kept quiet and thought, 'I think he has gone mad. Can't he see he is as old as twice me.' Then immediately, I went into a deep thought and decided that I should tell him "My brother is standing out there in the audience and in case he saw you speaking to me as your girlfriend, he would push you hard down on the ground." Then in a while, a roar rose from the audience. They wanted to know what I am going to say.

After that, my teachers forced me to say 'yes' to him. Suddenly, I came out of my thought process and with all my teacher's pressure, I said 'yes' to that old creature.

At the end of the program, the media gathered around me and took my interview asking me about my ambition.

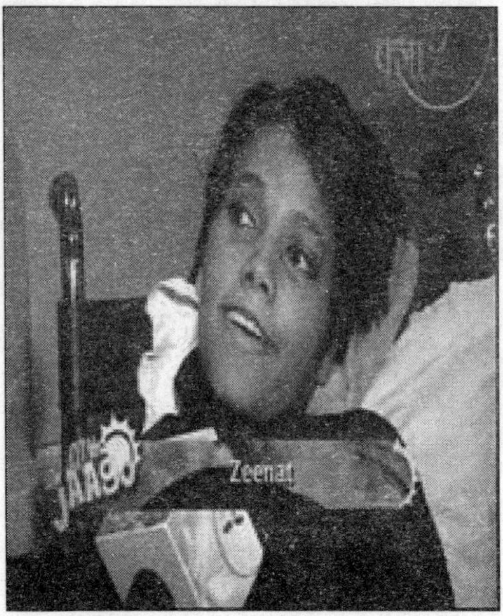

Zeenat giving her first interview at CSM Mall, Sector 18, Noida on Disabled Day.

It was a new experience for me. I had seen all this on TV before that. I never expected some day various media people would gather round me like flies, I couldn't understand what to speak when they asked me questions like: "Do I ever regret for being like this or do I blame God? Why have I selected fashion designing as my ambition?"

In the beginning, I felt nervous seeing the cameras flashing in front of me and besides this; they were asking me simultaneously. It was altogether a new experience for me. I had never done ever before in my life, and then immediately I gathered courage and spoke up. I said, "I never had any regret for anything I have received from God. Rather I feel proud that he selected me for all the biggest tests of life given by Him. If I pass the test, I will be rewarded the best."

And when they asked me about my ambition, I said "I have selected fashion designing as my ambition because, since my birth, my world was limited within the walls of my home, due to which I had developed a skill in me. It was whatever I would see around me, I would observe it deeply and try to make changes in their features, like if I see girls on TV, I would notice their bangles, suits, hairstyle, etc. and then try to improve upon them. In this way, I made my world more beautiful, more expandable."

□

40

10th Board Exams

I was very happy as my day went well, entirely different from the days I had spent so far. There was a big applause waiting for me. I didn't imagine that I would get such an unexpected welcome by people present at that event.

My heart was already filled with joy because of which I could concentrate on my studies better as I had to appear for my board exams a few weeks later.

I was giving my best in order to score good marks, even though in between my preparation, I got frequent chest congestion, deviating me from my aim. Along with preparation, I had tension about how I would be able to narrate things to my unknown writer because it is already a difficult task if a person has to complete his/her answer sheet within a given period of 3 hours and, in my case, I had to explain things to the other person, who might take more time in writing words. Besides this, if I wanted to change the position during the exam hour, whom I would have asked for. My life was very critical but I never took it in that sense. Instead I would always try to make it easy.

Just 2 weeks before my exams, my brother's application for being my writer was accepted, the only condition was that he had to pretend that he was one class junior to me.

Since my wish had been granted by Allah, I was very happy. Now I could have given my exam comfortably in the presence of my younger brother Mazhar. I never have had any regret for what Allah had done to me because He would always answer my prayers before more tears would have fallen down my eyes.

The day had approached when I had to appear for my first exam. I went with my brother Mazhar and did well as per my wish. I was blessed by Allah that all people, especially my family members, around me would always try to make sure that I didn't have any problem.

My brother who had done B.Arch. from AMU and was doing a job at that time, used to come home from office 2 hours before and then would take me to the exam centre. First he would take my wheelchair and place it where I would feel comfortable. In spite of its weight, he would do everything all alone, I was very lucky that I have got such loving and caring siblings as well as parents, who would always try their best to keep me happy.

During the exam hour, he would never let me take any sort of pain. He would feed me at frequent intervals, change my position as and when required. He would do so that I wouldn't feel exhausted and get ill. He was very careful about my health. He would consult a doctor before any mishap took place.

My sister Erum used to take me to hospital for a regular check-up since my brother would be in office. She took a very good care of mine during my illness. She used to give me medicine on time and since during my illness I had to cough out many times, both my siblings kept awake more often at night and would make me cough out. And if my brother was at home, he used to take me to hospital himself.

My last paper was science, the most awaited paper. I had prepared the theory portion but not the numerical portion. It was so because I was left with very little time and couldn't be able to practise numericals properly, although the teacher, Mrs. Neelam who taught me last, did her best and gave me preference over all students. She used to make other students get busy with some work and thus she managed to be free and so she gave all her spare time to me. In this way, she took my syllabus so fast that it had been completed on time. I am really very thankful to my creator who sent her at the end and she did whatever she could do to fulfill my requirement. I love that teacher as well as respect her a lot.

When the exams got over, the same night I thought of Sameer Sir. He had said to me when he used to teach me, "You will definitely score 90 percent marks in science. I will prepare you that way." Now I realised why I was facing a problem in understanding things when he used to teach me. It was because he was teaching me from the guide as I wasn't provided with the books from the NIOS board, from which I had proceeded for my class 10th.

In the guide, things are not given in detail, due to which sometimes people feel difficulty in getting a detailed information.

□

41
Zeenat Scores Good Marks

I was lying down on the bed and searching for my result on the internet in my cell phone since morning. I was eagerly waiting for the outcome for which I worked hard one month before. Once I put my enrolment number in the search box, my eyes automatically got closed as I was expecting 90 percent marks but, when I found out the result, it was 71 percent overall. I was not satisfied with the marks because I believed I would get more than it was showing in the mark-sheet. I felt low-hearted until I found my parents overjoyed. They told me, "You have scored the best marks, dear. What more did you expect? It is difficult to score such good marks by normal people and in your case, there were numerous limitations and still you did well, dear."

It was true. I scored excellent marks along with one of the biggest challenges of my life. I required one's help at every second of my life. Even then, I studied hard and had not done bad.

After some time, I felt I scored well and I should not worry about it much. Rather I should go ahead and share this amazing news with other people far away. I happily took my cell phone, contacted all numbers whom I was wishing to tell this news. I called all relatives as well as teachers close to me. When everyone got to know that news, they were happier than I was myself.

I saw that there was Sameer Sir's number in my cell. I thought I should let him also know about the result. So I called on his number and to my luck, it had connected to him quickly. When he picked up the phone, he was very surprised. He never expected I would ever call him again, although he turned out to be very happy listening to my voice after a long time.

I said that I had scored not up to his expectation but instead had scored 71 percent. On hearing that, he was very happy and said to me, "You did your best and could do more ahead in life." He said sorry for not being able to continue my classes as he had to go for his training during that period. He told me that he got placed in HYUNDAI just after going through the training and was in Chennai.

When I said sorry to him for having misbehaved during our classes, he said, "Forget all about it. I never took it hard and we both are good friends. Please stop treating me like a teacher. I am your friend." At this, I smiled, my respect for him had increased greatly.

□

42

Future Planning was Done

I was very happy because I was over with my class 10thand was planning to do fashion designing as my age was more at that time. I should have been doing my bachelors when I had completed class 10th and this delay was due to my physical health. If I were able to sit properly without any support, I would have gone in a regular school and completed my studies on time.

I wanted to do some diploma course so that I could start earning as soon as possible. Although I could not move myself but I had the dedication of living a normal life. That's why, I wanted to start earning soon. People, when they cross 23 years and complete their studies, prefer to earn money, I also had the same thought.

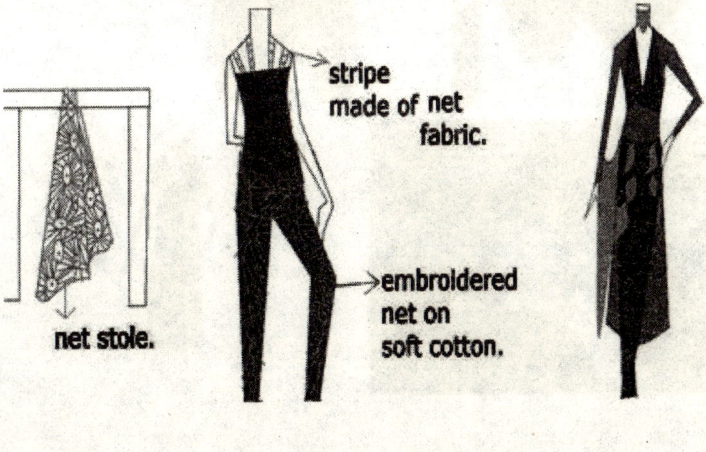

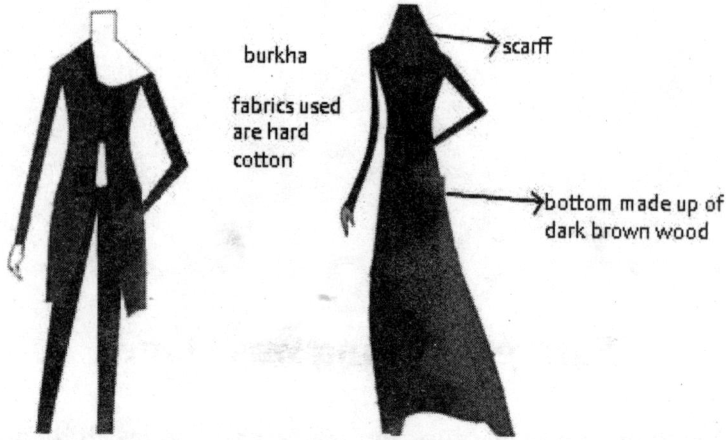
burkha
fabrics used are hard cotton
scarff
bottom made up of dark brown wood

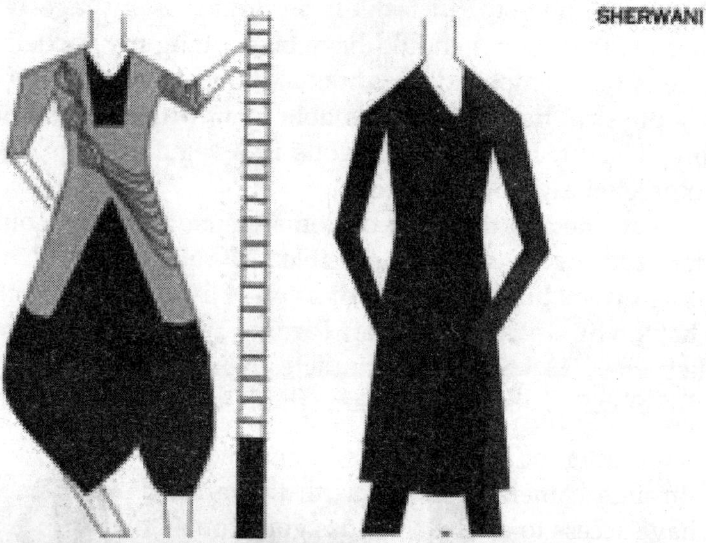
SHERWANI

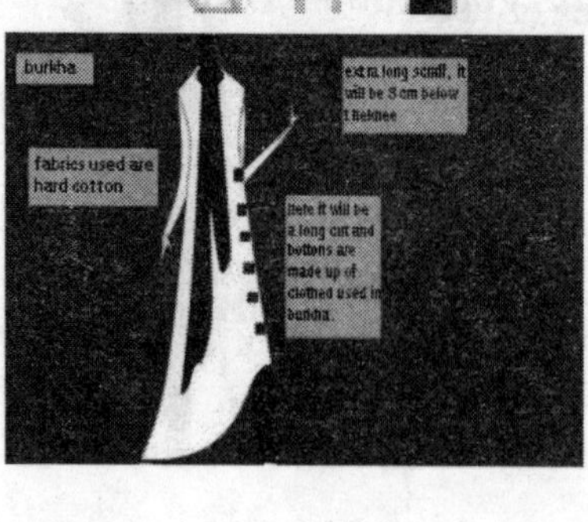
burkha
fabrics used are hard cotton

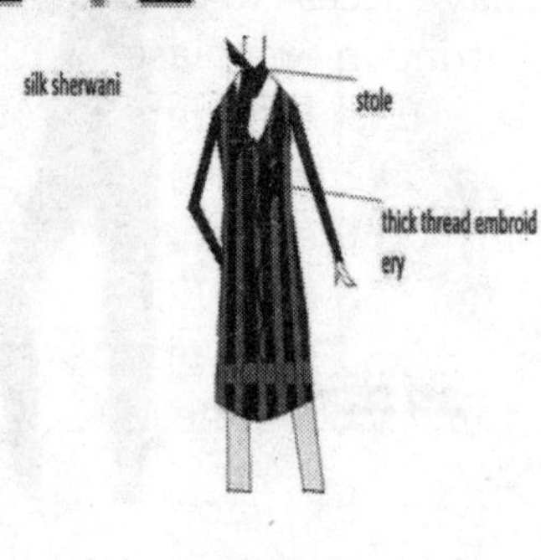
silk sherwani
stole
thick thread embroid ery

Dresses designed by Zeenat.

I planned that after completing the course in fashion designing, I would open a small boutique that would gradually turn into a big fashion house – a fashion house with different activity areas, connected with my computer through cameras. And so with this arrangement, I could have access to all the activities going outside my office just sitting in one place.

First I thought I would go for the diploma course that was available in some institute near my home, but later, my brother and sister suggested to me that I should first complete class 12th and then think of doing any other course.

So, I gave priority to my siblings' word and joined the same school, the MBCN after the vacation.

□

43

Zeenat Starts having Frequent Troubles

Life was going smoothly and I entered class 12th.Although this time I had planned to give exams in installments like I had a choice of completing class 12th in 5 years by giving one paper a year, but despite all that, I would have completed it in just one year if my health did not create problems often.

My studies went well and again I came close to my board exams. This time my brother Mazhar would take me to the exam centre, same as he used to, very carefully. This time also he would come 2 hours before my exam started. I only had given two papers that year, Economics and English, and left the three other papers, business studies, accountancy and home science for the coming year. By doing so, I had avoided extra burden on me, keeping my heath in a good shape. Actually, had I given all papers at a time, I would have to spend all my energy and due to which I could fall ill.

□

44

A Feeling of Insecurity

Now my age was 24 years and I became more mature than before. I understood that life is not a play which ends up in loss to one side and victory to another. Instead, it continues with daily problems and ends up with life of the person.

I realised how difficult my living would be at the stage when both of my siblings got married and my parents became old. Then who would take care of me? My siblings would have their own life, busy with their own family, their needs, likes and dislikes.

That feeling surrounded me such that I would always put a 'question' before God, "Why did you, Allah, not make me like others?" And soon my eyes would fill with tears.

□

45

God Answered Me in an Unpredictable Way

That insecurity was eating me up badly. I was not able to feel calm and relaxed. I used to feel so irritated inside that I could not sleep sometimes the whole night.

Whenever there was no one around me, I would find my eyes wet in tears. Those teary eyes speak to Allah in silence, "Why have you not made somebody for me who could look after me throughout my life?"

It was a true feeling, what I felt, that even a normal girl who is independent, who earns her own livelihood, requires someone's support, under whose influence she could feel comfortable.

Days passed rapidly like the wind around us and so my sense of insecurity was also increasing. And truly one would have felt the same way as I felt because it is very difficult to live life with a smile on when you can't even move yourself an inch of your own wish.

It was Ramadan time when I got ill. My condition became so terrible that I had difficulty in breathing. Fortunately, my brother was at home that day and so he took me to the nearest hospital quickly. He was so much disquieted that he was not able to hold up himself. That is why, he took Adil, our neighbour along to the hospital. Adil was our neighbour in name only but he was more than a neighbour for my family, especially for me, he was nothing less than my own brother Mazhar.

They took me to the Bhardwaj Hospital, Sector 29, Noida near my home, where Dr. Bhardwaj immediately treated me. He was a very good doctor and easy to reach, used to treat me since I was a child. He used to treat me very carefully just like a fragile baby. He would never take any risk in my case. He would try all the possible ways to restore my good health. I would also follow his advice very sincerely.

Zeenat with her brother Mazhar Husain and Adil Khan on her birthday.

He examined me, prescribed medicine and then both of them, Mazhar and Adil took me back in the car. My sister Erum was also with them. She was holding me in her lap. Her condition was also getting worse at seeing me. Actually my siblings loved me a lot, maybe more than what I actually knew.

They took me straight back home where my mother eagerly waited for me. When I reached, my mother ran towards my brother with a heavy heart and snatched me from his grip. This time also my condition was not seen properly. I was breathing heavily. My mother gave me medicines immediately. I should have a little relief, but instead of getting a relief, my problem worsened. I was barely able to take a breath. There was darkness before my eyes. Everyone got horrified at seeing me. All three present at home were crying badly. By that time, Adil had left for his home.

My brother called Adil to come back again and take me to hospital immediately because he was very stressed and so was not in a condition to take me alone.

They reached the hospital on time. I had been given oxygen and other relaxing mechanisms. Dr. Bhardwaj diagnosed me with pneumonitis. He told Mazhar that they were giving me nebuliser filled with effective medicine, which would help to remove mucus accumulated in my lungs through faeces and urine, due to which I was unable to breathe properly.

Since I had SMA, I had to keep myself safe from all types of infection, because due to weakened muscles of all body parts, sometimes it became difficult to recover such infections in lungs.

Everyone sitting around me in the hospital room found me a little calm as now oxygen was going through my nostrils continuously.

At night the same day, a new doctor came on a visit to examine me. His name was Dr. Vivek Goswami. Actually Dr. Bhardwaj had to go somewhere else urgently. So, he let my treatment continue under him till he was back and besides this, he wanted to have a second opinion of a paediatrician since my weight was little, approximately 20 kg.

The doctor entered my room and took off the blanket, which was over me, asking people standing around my bed, "I want to know the history first. I mean how she eats, sits, etc. I want to know her overall lifestyle." At this, everyone lowered their heads as they didn't have the idea of my disease I was born with, and my father was out of station, who knew the name of the disease. So, my sister Erum standing nearby, who had once heard from a physiotherapist at my school speaking about my problem, said, "Doctor, she is having muscular dystrophy and we give her food after keeping her head at some height, like putting pillows under her head so that she can easily chew." Before she could speak further, I interrupted, "No, doctor, I am not having muscular dystrophy, I am having SMA." Soon the doctor turned to me. He could not believe his eyes seeing my courage while being in such a stiff condition. He was amazed because I was barely able to breathe. Still I collected strength and defended the wrong happening to me.

He smiled and removed the nebuliser mask from my face, he stared at me awhile and then said, "SMA what type?" I said, "2." He didn't keep his eyes away from my sight till he was present in that room and then finally he said, "I must say she is very sweet." Soon after, he left.

That time my father was out of station and my brother and sister did for me, maybe more than my parents would have done for me.

My sister Erum, who was doing B.Tech. from AMITY, Noida, left all her papers, term paper and would stay with me at hospital all day and night. She didn't sleep many nights during that period. She would take a very good care of me and with the passage of time, my mother was able to go back home and complete all household work, since she was satisfied with me being with Erum. On the other side, my brother was putting in all his effort, so that his sister could have the best treatment and get back to my original state soon.

He would come to hospital straight from office. Then both of them, my sister and brother, would talk long to the doctor under whom my treatment was going. Whenever my mouth would get filled with cough fluid, both of them would change my position, turn me to a side so that my cough released out easily.

During that period, both my siblings did a lot for me that I was able to know I am blessed with such a caring and loving brother and sister and wish to Allah that everyone could have siblings like them.

I could not believe that Allah would ever answer my question so nicely. My sense of insecurity of being alone at the time when my parents would become old seemed to be getting over. By now, I knew my siblings will accord me top priority even if they got married.

□

46
Quick Recovery

I always believed that if Allah wants something to happen, then there is no power on this earth or anything in this universe that could stop it to happen. In the same way, if Allah wants nothing wrong should happen to me, I will definitely come out of that mishap unscathed.

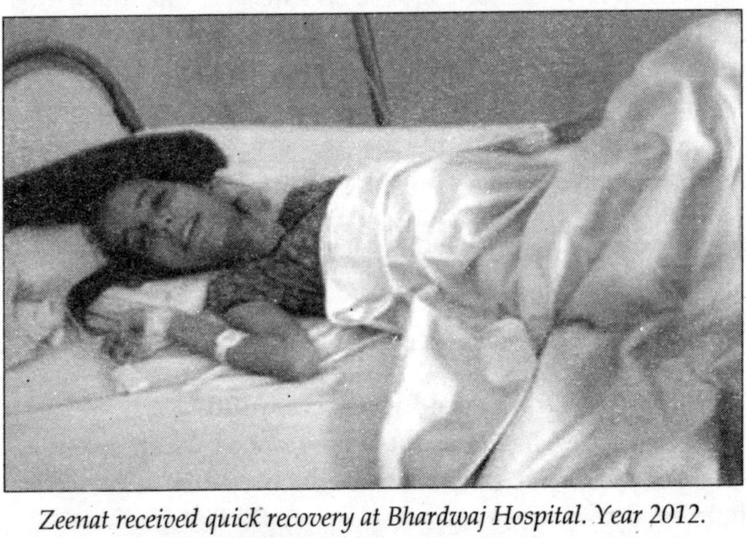

Zeenat received quick recovery at Bhardwaj Hospital. Year 2012.

And so, the same thing happened I received a quick recovery. My right lung got cleared the next day of my admission in the hospital.

Dr. Vivek came into my room the next day, my brother and sister were also there, and he checked me and found my recovery so fast. He was very happy to see my condition getting normal at such a fast pace, he didn't expect that earlier.

Actually, I was very weak and didn't have the strength to cough out strongly, in that case the mucus accumulated in my lungs wouldn't easily release out, due to which Dr. Vivek previously had recommended to put me on the ventilator but later on, he realised that I was internally very strong.

All the doctors coming on visit would praise my attitude towards life, especially Dr. Vivek. Some doctors even gave me compliments for my beauty. They would say how beautifully I smiled. One of the doctors, whose name was Ishtiyak, even compared my smile with the actress in Sanjay Leela Bhansali's movie and others said that I was very pretty. In short, I got compliments after compliments from here and there in the whole of hospital. One of the doctors, whose name was Sunil, was very appreciative. I got the best compliment from him. He said, "You are the most important person on this earth, just keep smiling always."

All these praises and positive approach raised my moral higher than ever before. Now I would think I was not only anything for this world, but I was everything for this world.

Time to Get Discharged from Hospital

Now it had been almost 5 days since I was in hospital. Everyday Dr. Vivek would come on a visit and seeing my improved recovery every time, he would feel good inside.

It was the last day of my discharge. The doctor entered my room. Now I too had got a little strength to speak with him. My net-book was kept next to me. So, the doctor said, "Umm…so Zeenat using internet!"

I said, "No, doctor, actually my sister was feeling bored up, so she brought it to watch movies."

Then my doctor asked my sister about my likes and dislikes. She said to him, "Doctor, she is a very good designer. She wears clothes designed by herself and she goes to the mall to buy dresses for herself. She is very choosy and black is her favourite colour. And another thing is that you must see her designs, they are on her laptop."

Then she showed him all my designs. Between this she kept speaking continuously letting him know that his patient Zeenat was something special. She always searches about her disease on the net and collects all negative things regarding her problem, which can later harass her. She requested him to try to talk to me and remove all my negative thoughts from my mind.

Between their talks, his eyes were stuck fast at me. He seemed to be in a deep thought. However, I noticed it but I never tried to know the reason behind. Maybe he might have thought that God had given me numerous strength.

Once Erum finished with her talk, the doctor turned to me and asked leaning towards me, "Zeenat, are you on the Facebook?" He knew if somebody uses the net, he/she must be on the Facebook (a social networking site) as well. At this, I answered 'yes'. He took my id at once and added me as his friend at the same moment on his cellphone and then he came close to my ears and said, "You look so beautiful, change your profile picture." There was a blush on his face. He was smiling endlessly and soon after, he discharged me after he had examined me thoroughly.

I never knew I could ever meet such a nice human in the form of doctor. I felt that he was treating me without any return. He was very much into my case selflessly.

But it is also true that no one does things without any return in this world. If somebody has done hard work for 5 to 6 years in medical, he/she will definitely expect some return. It was only my thought. I was good by heart. So, I used to see the same quality in others.

He just put in all his efforts to bring me in a normal state. Allah had given me in the right hand. I was fortunate that he had started treating me when Dr. Bhardwaj handed me over to him during his absence.

I remember that after my discharge, my doctor prescribed me medicines for five days, after which I had to go for the check-up, but when I went next, he was on leave. My sister called him letting him know that I was in hospital and it won't be easy for her to bring me again and again. Before she could speak further, he said, "I'll be there in five minutes." And he came especially for me.

Generally, it never happens. If a doctor is on leave, he or she never comes. I had this type of experience before with other doctors. But with him, it was different. He was a true noble doctor. Allah had sent him as an angel for me for the time being.

I was very happy because I was going to live a healthy life same as before. I gave a big thanks to Allah and kept it firm inside me that I shall never let smile go off my face. In any case, that he Allah, the biggest power is always there with me.

And that was not the end of that beautiful girl. There were more challenges left. She was supposed to face but, I, Zeenat going to take you out of her world for a while. It's time for you now to have some break.

Thanks

Think positive with a firm faith in your god. You can feel how your life becomes easy even when numerous problems prevail over you.

Three upcoming characters of my next book – DM of Noida, Mr. N.P. Singh, who gave a new direction to my life; Master Parth Malhotra and Dr. Ashish Jaiswal.

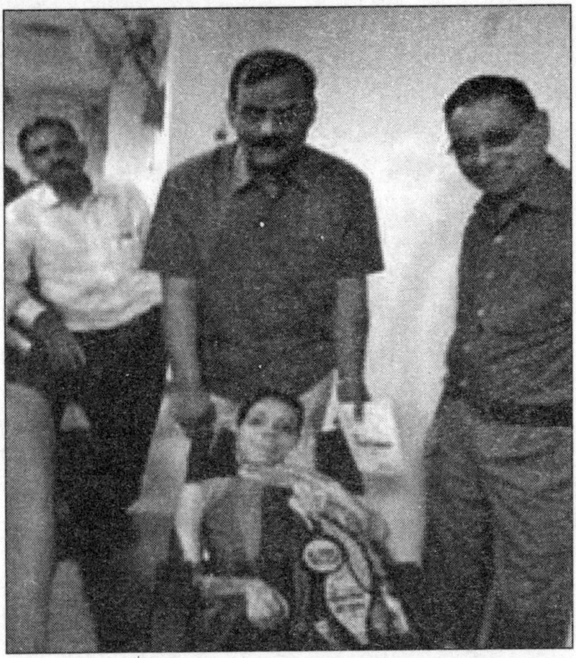

Zeenat with DM of Noida, N.P. Singh received award for the brave girl.

Zeenat with her rabbit Parth Malhotra.

Sanskruti correspondence course of **Interior Design** Basic consists of two manuals, which professionally cover all the basic subjects on interior designing, beside aspects of general interest. The course duration is 12 months.

Sanskruti correspondence course of Interior Design Advanced consists of three manuals which, besides the fundamental subjects, contained in the Basic course covers, in Manual 3, information on new materials, new furniture types, new residential and office trends, drafting guidelines, heritage restoration, details of concepts and compositions, professional practice and colour styles, besides advancements in lighting and air conditioning field. The course duration is 15 months.

The manuals contain over 650 diagrams, tables, sketches and photographs in colour, covering fascinating subjects which give career level knowledge.

The course emphasises the 'FUNDAMENTALS OF INTERIOR DESIGN' which can be of great benefit to the aspiring students. If the fundamentals are well understood, work experience or further studies can strengthen a professional's career.

Sanskruti Manuals are the only reference books on Interior Design recommended by The Directorate of Technical Education, Maharashtra, India to all colleges.

I told you, my readers, that after entering my world, you would like to enter it again and again. It's very interesting to explore one's life, to know how he/she struggled to finally reach the goal, but it is very difficult to sit with him/her and share the pain together. Your pain, your crisis can only be shared by Allah and no one else. People will always gather around you in your happiness, but in your pain, you will find your Creator (Allah) only, and no one else. This is the truth of life.

So, my readers, as now you have entered my world again, I want to share with you an experience of my life which I felt as a child. I am telling you about my world from my first addition. I know you must be in confusion to know that how could my world be different when Allah (god) has given us birth in the same world.

As a child, I also had the same thought which gradually turned into a mature thought with the passage of time. When I opened my eyes in your world, I found myself very different and the people of your world also always tried to make me sure that I am not like them, I don't have the rights as they have just because my physical ability is not like theirs. My feelings, my desires merely don't make any sense that I can go along with them together in the run of life. I thought in isolation if there is a vast difference between my world and the world in which you people exist, I will definitely turn my world superior to yours. A beautiful world which could be the dream of a single normal person, which is sometimes not developed even after putting the best of efforts by a human.

I thought, maybe it was the reason why God has created me physically different from others to show you people that everything is in the hand of Him (God), and not yours. If you divided His world into two parts, leaving me alone in one of those, that doesn't mean I will give my life an end in a fear to cover the distance created by this worldly people between two worlds, rather He (God) made it more beautiful, creating the desire in people to reach it.

He (Allah) has made my world so tough enabling me to achieve that everyone only dreams to reach where I am today.

By saying all this, I don't mean that I am the most intelligent person in this world, who only has the ability to create such a dream world, but I would like to say that your world is full of brilliant people in front of whom my intelligence stands nowhere, but then also, they lack somewhere to reach their dreams.

I don't know why being so intelligent, they lack to understand the divine power all the time. Their biggest fault is that they don't have faith on their Creator, who has created all universe and all that is in it. This is the weakest point in people due to which they sometimes suffer in this world or hereafter. I have seen some people in my friends' circle and relatives who were brilliant but they never reached where they should be according to their intelligence. Whenever I see them, I get confused why it is so. I mean they had a treasure of knowledge, still they were far behind.

Later, I realised their partial faith on the Designer of this world is the biggest reason they never reached where they should be.

At seeing this, my faith became firmer and I started believing that I am more intelligent because I found the real strength of God who helped me in all odds of life and I will always keep this belief in my heart that He will definitely make my life better. Insha Allah!

And, so my readers, I will not take much of your time, I will take you ahead from where I had left you in my story.

As I introduced you with three new people of my life in my first edition, in this book you will get to know about them in brief:

DM of Noida, Mr. Nagendra Pratap Singh. I really respect him as much as I respect my parents. Allah has given him the ability to read what is in my heart.

Dr. Ashish (pulmonologist) never treated me as a doctor. I always found in him a good friend.

Parth (my rabbit) what should I tell you about him, I love him the most.

□

47

Link Between Two Doors

After being in hospital for five days, it felt like I entered into a new life. I was very happy because I was feeling very fresh, more than ever before.

In the same year in the month of November 2012, my heart was attracted towards a baby, who was living just next to my balcony. Actually his main door was in front of my balcony's door. In my home, there was a way to go downstairs from the balcony also. His kitchen window was also opened in my balcony.

I saw him properly in the month of November, when I was sitting in my balcony along with my mother. His main door was open and our balcony's door was also open. I saw him in his mother's lap through it. My mother approached him. At this, his Mom brought him close to us and said to the child, "Say hello to Aunty." In the meanwhile, he enjoyed our company. So, his Mom made him stand down the floor and brought his toys and asked him to play with us.

I still remember that day. It was very cold and my Mom saw the sunlight. So, she had brought me out. He enjoyed a lot playing with us. My Mom tried to bring him in the balcony because it was very cold and he stood in the space which would divide his main door and my balcony's door. But he would neither come this side nor go that side, I mean inside his home. He just stared at both of us, and when we both would go inside, he would start crying.

Again I would say it was Allah's plan that I met him. He had all the qualities which I was missing since long back. Although I would never say anything to anyone at home, but my eyes would always search the baby Saif in all children known to me in my family, friends and relatives.

But I found those qualities next to my balcony door, in Parth.

After that first meeting, everyday I would sit in the balcony to have sunlight. He would too stand in the space between two doors and showing the shapes would say (Mummy Bua) it was a square, and that was a circle. Actually, at that time, he was just two years old due to which he used to stammer and could not clearly speak my nickname (Manni).

One day, I didn't go out in the balcony to sit in sunlight. Only Mummy was out. When he didn't find me out, he straightaway came inside my home for the first time, and looked for me here and there. When Erum (my sister) saw this act of a small baby, she showed him the room I was sleeping in. He instantly came and put his sweet hand on my face and said, "Mummy Bua, *utho* (rise), Manni Bua, wake up."

From that day, he started coming to my home everyday. First he came twice a day, then thrice a day, and then there was no limit. He would come any time. There was no time boundation. In fact, he became like a part of my family. He was attached not only to me but also to my whole family.

I should share an incident with you....

One day in the afternoon, he came and I don't remember exactly what had happened. Erum shouted on him, not intentionally but to see his reaction. He shouted equally back on her but when I said that this was wrong and shouted on him, he could not bear with it. He started crying badly as if someone had hurt his feelings because he never expected that from me, even if he had done the biggest crime in this world.

He was just two-and-a-half old, but believe me, when he would see Mummy or Erum helping me in any work, like when helping me to hold the glass of milk. He would take it from my hand and pour it into my mouth very accurately, maybe more accurately than the elders.

He knew everything related to me. How I take food, how I sit in my wheelchair. Since my wheelchair was customised, he knew its arrangement very well.

One day in the evening, I was sitting in my balcony, he was also there. My father was trying to make my wheelchair stand in a position but he was unable to do so. Parth said, "Abbu, just get aside." Actually, he used to call my father Abbu as I and my siblings used to call.

The moment Abbu stood up on the other side, he came close to my wheelchair and put breaks on. He knew each and everything about my wheelchair arrangements.

Whenever I would feel lonely in this big world, he would bring smile on my face. It was true that I never take my life difficult, but that doesn't mean there was no pain. Sometimes, when I sit in peace, I would feel like I am surrounded with darkness and that darkness was supposed to eat me up if I failed to find light. Then my Parth baby would climb up my wheelchair with his small feet and would say putting his cute hands on my face, "Bua, don't take tension, everything will be alright." He would become a ray of light and hope, and wake me up from my thoughts.

□

48

A Relation Made by God

Parth was a person whom my eyes would always search, whenever darkness engulfed me, that was following me since my birth. When it would try to swallow me in it, it was Parth's stammering voice that would bring me back in light again.

He brought many happy moments in my life. I started seeing Saif in him and the most amazing thing was he would resemble a lot to him. I would feel very happy if he was around me. My pain would diminish when he would say, "Manni Bua, why do you take tension? I will take you to my home and keep you with me always. I will feed you and make you sleep next to me. Whenever you would need help, I will wake up." It was these lines uttered by a three-year-old kid. He would speak more sincerely than a grown-up person.

It was the year 2013 when I got ill again in the month of March. The symptoms were the same as before, but severity was less.

When my brother Mazhar came from office, he saw that I was having difficulty in coughing out. He asked me if I was having a little trouble, I should let him know, so he would take me to hospital at once. He would never take risk in my case. He never waited for my condition to get worse. Both my sister and brother were very caring for my health.

They took me to the same hospital I used to go since my birth, Bhardwaj where I had been treated by Dr. Vivek Goswami. Now my treatment would go under him only because his medicine worked on me when I was admitted first time.

When he examined me, he found out there was nothing serious, but since I was very nervous, he recommended me to be under medical observation for at least two days. When he came next day in the morning for a check-up, I told him I was feeling excessive congestion in my left lung. Actually I was very weak. So, I couldn't understand whether I got relief or not. In that case, I usually made him panic. He increased antibiotics dosage and then I faced its side effects. My lungs got a proper relief but it felt to me as if my system was not supporting my desire to live. I even shared this to all doctors who came on round, including Dr. Vivek. They said, "It's all because of increased dosage of antibiotics. The moment its impact was decreased, you will get relief slowly."

In this way, I stayed in hospital for six days. When Parth did not see me, he would ask everybody, "Where is Manni Bua? At least tell me where she is?"

When my sister Erum would tell him that Dr. Goswami is not letting your Bua to come, he usually got angry and take anything kept nearby to pretend as if he is talking to Dr. Vivek on phone and would say, "Hello, Dr. Goswami, if you do not let my Bua come back, I will give you a slap." Actually, he knew him well because his mother used to take him to the same doctor in case he fell ill.

He was so much attached to me that in my absence, he would go to my home less frequently.

When I came back from hospital, he came close to me and started playing with me. He said, "Bua, please don't go anywhere." I said, "Why, baby, Bua was not well, that's why she went to hospital to get treatment. Now your Bua has come back." At this, he said, "No, I miss you a lot because I love you." When his mother came to take him, she said, "Manni, what magic you have done on him. He is so happy since morning, it is wonder what treasure he has got after meeting you." At this I smiled. I would not comment on anything.

He would speak so cutely that sometimes I couldn't believe that they were really the words of a three-year-old kid. One day, he was leaving for his Nana's place. Before leaving anywhere, he would visit me. So, when he came, he said to me, "Manni Bua, I am going to my Nanu's place for a few days. Please don't take tension. I will come soon. Actually, one of my cousins over there misses me too. He says: Parth Bhaiya, please come to me too. So, you just don't take tension. I will come soon and if Saba Bua or anybody hurts you, do let me know. I will not let them go so easily."

After that, he talked to my sister as well. He said, "Saba, in my absence, you have to do everything Manni tells you. Give her evening tea on time by keeping her pillow properly below her neck and cover up her head whenever she recites namaz and listen to her whenever she calls anybody in need. If I get any complaint from Manni, I will beat you with my hands."

When I would listen to a big talk of a small kid, I would start feeling good and all my pain would vanish into the sky. He would speak so sincerely that it would make me feel that he is the most concerned person for me in this world.

You can't believe he knew each and everything about me. He had the knowledge about what clothes I have, what pieces of jewellery I have, he knew each and every belonging of mine. One day, I had a desire of having momos, Parth asked his Mom, "Mummy, please give one mamose to Manni Bua. She doesn't eat much, she eats a little." But his Mom told him, "Beta, all is over now. We will buy for Manni Bua next time."

Next day in the evening, when he came to meet me, he said, "Erum, please take me to the momos shop. I feel like eating it." When he went there, he didn't eat a single momos. Instead he asked her to give an order to pack them all for home. In a while, they reached home. He ran towards me and climbed up my wheelchair and said, "My Manni Bua wanted eating it. Just because I went to buy it, I was not feeling like to eat it. Now my Manni is happy."

He was just a small kid, 4 years old, but his thoughts were far superior to that of these worldly people. He gave priority to my happiness over everything else, whereas in this world, people are so selfish that even if they do something for you, they will like to draw indirect benefit for them, and here was a small kid who gave importance just to my happiness. His thoughts were beyond the humans' imagination.

The moment which I spent with him will always be the moment which I prefer to live again and again in my life. Whenever I would take a bath and if that moment he was present at my home, he would come close to my bed and would say by smelling my hair, "Wow! Manni Bua is looking so beautiful. Bua, why did you wear this dress? It doesn't look good on you."

I miss those cute little moments so much. When my sister used to pretend as if she was beating me with her hands in front of him, he would immediately run towards my sister and pull her away from me and then would surround me with his cute hands in such a way that no one could touch me.

What more should I tell you about him? If I start telling you about his involvement in my life and all the happy moments which I spent with him, the space in this book will not suffice for others. I still remember his touching words he used to tell me whenever I pretended to get annoyed with him, "MANNI, I COME TO MEET YOU WITH DIFFICULTY, PLEASE TALK TO ME." When he would say that, tears would start streaming out of my eyes. I don't know why he used to say that.

One day I was lying down on the bed when he came to me and said, "What happened to your hand, Manni Bua? Who has spoiled your hand?" Actually, I had the marks of pricking niddles in my hand due to the intravenous injections that the doctor prescribed me for a few days.

When I said, "Baby, Uncle gave injection to your Bua so that Bua gets well soon and then play with Parth," at that, he said, "I will not leave that guy who spoiled my Bua's hand. I will tie him to the ceiling fan with a rope."

□

49
Exam Time

Now only three papers were left for me to complete my class 12th: home science, business studies and accountancy.

After recovering from illness, I started preparing for my exams, which were in April. I thought I would give only two papers that year: home science and business studies because very little time was left, only two weeks. Actually, I fell ill in the first week of March and my paper was in the second week of April the same year of 2013. So, the time for preparing for exams was very short, and in between, I needed to regain my strength which I had lost during my fight with the illness.

Although it was very tough to do two things simultaneously, to regain strength and study for exams, for a girl who couldn't do anything of her own, except imagining things how to perform them.

But then I decided I would not leave these two papers because they both were theoretical and I had already completed my syllabus before my illness had ensued. So, what I did was to ask people around me to keep a pillow on my stomach and then my book over it. In this way, I could go through all the chapters and could try to memorise whatever I could.

Since I couldn't write a single alphabet with the pen due to lack of movement in my hands, nor could I ask someone to make notes because, as I told you earlier, you have no control over others, you have it only over yourself. So, whenever I asked someone to make it, I would find them busy and you can't pressurise others. You could continuously ask God for a thing and He listens to you sooner or later, but you can't continuously ask these worldly people or else they get irritated of you. So is not the case with God.

So, this was how I had to read and study the entire chapters.

When exam time came, my sister Erum went with me tc write the paper, but this time we were not prepared properly. Actually, every time I had to apply for a writer to write for me, but due to my illness, that time I forgot to tell my siblings about it.

When we entered the exam hall, they asked my sister about the application. She told them everything. At this, they said they will provide their own writer, but the moment they understood my requirements, like my sister informed them about my frequent changing positions, my requirement to drink liquid at frequent intervals, they agreed to allow my sister to write my paper for me.

But, again a problem came. They said that they will not let her sit in the next paper unless she did not bring the writer's application issued by the NIOS of the board.

One week had gone but no one got time to bring the writer's application and when only one day was left for my examination, my brother Mazhar told me that I should appear in my remaining papers next year, which could be business studies and accountancy, although my preparation for business studies was good. So, I skipped the examinations just by believing it as God's will.

□

50
Frequent Hospitalisation

Now my immunity became weaker. I got ill more frequently than before. Even a small change in weather would not suit me. Actually, my muscles were getting weaker day by day, due to which I was losing power to fight the disease.

As I have already given you information about my inborn disease SMA, in which a patient's life span depends on his/her respiratory care, maybe I was not getting that care in the right way, because it involves proper education related to the disease, which somewhere in my family possibly lacked. I was not aware about it until I read about it on the net. When I gathered information regarding this problem, I tried to make my family educated in this area. I had little knowledge, but whatever I learnt from the internet, I tried to implement it in my lifestyle.

My motive behind writing this book is also to make people aware about this disease who are little educated in this area. I want of all parents that they should give utmost priority to their children's respiratory system in order to give their children a healthy life.

These children should be kept under a stable temperature. Wherever they go, the temperature should be maintained. Their eating habits should also be taken into consideration in order to give a good shape to their muscles. Their diet should involve more protein in broken form (amino acids) so that the muscles could absorb it completely. Lung therapy is a must, whether in mechanical or physical form. The children should be taken to nutrition experts from time to time, and secondly, a patient with SMA should not be kept in lying position all the time. Instead his or her body should be in a motion most of the time, like he should move from one place to another more often. This is what I experienced and this gave me relief and comfort. In this way, his mind will get a chance to explore new things, which will increase his desire to live and when his body is in motion, cough wouldn't accumulate inside the lungs.

So, now coming to the main point, it was the time when I got ill in the month of November in the same year 2013 again. I got admitted in the first week of November. That time, both my parents were out. They had gone to Mumbai to meet some relative. Just two days after they left, I suffered from influenza due to seasonal change. My condition became very worse, so I needed medical assistance at once. My brother Mazhar took me to the same hospital where Dr. Vivek recommended me to keep me in hospital for two days, although my recovery used to take more time and I stayed there for six days instead.

Every time my normal infection turned into pneumonia, it generally took time to recover. It was very easy for the doctor to experiment different antibiotics on me to get rid of the infection, but it was more difficult for me to support the medicine to fight the bacterias inside my lungs because when I would fully recover and collect some strength, I again got ill.

But believe me, my readers, my breath was alive with the belief that no power is stronger than the divine power and so, every time I defeated my illness.

Dr. Vivek had put me on a combination of two antibiotics: MONOCEF and VANCOMYCIN. My infection had spread so much that antibiotics were working very slowly and it took five days to completely clear my infection.

On the fifth day, when doctor came on round in the evening time, I told him a lie in order to get discharged from the hospital.

Actually, my mother was having difficulty in managing both hospital and home simultaneously. So, with this fact in mind, I lied to him, although he didn't want me to be discharged until the completion of antibiotics dosage. He didn't want to keep me on oral medication because those days it wasn't working on me.

At the time of discharge, vancomycin course was not completed, the doctor wanted me to complete it but I didn't listen to him because of my home situation.

□

51

The Longest Stay of My Life in Hospital

When the doctor discharged me before completion of the antibiotics course and kept me on oral medication, the infection reoccurred within one week. By that time, my parents were also back from Mumbai.

When my sister Erum took me to the doctor's clinic in Sector 30, he said, "I had told you earlier that the antibiotics course wasn't completed because of which she is not responding to oral medication. That might be the reason for the recurrence of the infection."

The good thing was that I used to get medical assistance at once when I got ill. No delay at all would take place because both hospitals and my doctor's clinic were at a five minutes' distance from my home in Sector 37.

After examining me, he prescribed me the same antibiotics and asked my sister to get me admitted in the hospital and start IV (intravenous) as soon as possible, but at this, my sister told him if they could give IV at home because her exams were drawing near and it wouldn't be possible for her family to manage hospitalisation so frequently.

The doctor agreed for this but asked her that there should not be any delay in the medication.

When we reached home, we contacted many nurses who could attend me at night as well because antibiotics needed to be injected four to five times a day, but nobody's schedule was matching with my requirements.

I was feeling terribly tight in my left lung, that's why I asked the doctor whether I should go for a pulmonologist. At this, he said, "You don't need any pulmonologist. You only need antibiotics." But I don't know how after some time, he recommended me to a pulmonologist in the same hospital, Bhardwaj.

It was the same pulmonologist about whom my sister had already searched on the internet. His name was Dr. Ashish Jaiswal. He used to pay home visits also. When my sister called on his number and explained my problem to him, he came to see me.

He was sitting in a couch next to the bed I was lying down on. He saw all my x-ray reports and compared them, I could see disappointment on his face. It felt to me from his face that we have delayed the case somewhere. Later he called Dr. Vivek and said, "Her left lung is gone". At that he said, "No, you are not able to locate her left lung because she has scoliosis." When he heard this, I saw a different expression on his face, he seemed to be satisfied.

Then he suggested me that before going with any antibiotics, I should go for a test which is called bronchoscopy. With this test, the cause of recurrence could be detected.

Since in this test they use a plastic tube which is inserted through the nostril into the lungs, which created fear inside me, so I directly said no to this procedure. I asked the doctor, "Please go with some other procedure if there is any possibility."

He made me satisfied by saying, "Zeenat, don't worry, we will first go with city scan, and then, if needed, will go for bronchoscopy."

My mummy offered him tea and coffee. He accepted the offer and said, "Aunty, where do you people belong to?"

I don't know why he asked this, maybe he must have noticed some clue in our way of speaking. When my mother said 'Faizabaad', he smiled and said, "Aunty, it's my native place as well."

From that day, he never used to treat me as a patient. Although he himself was a great person, he would never bring his profession into humanity.

Next day at night, my condition started growing worse. I didn't let my mother and sister go to sleep the whole night. I can't explain you how difficult it was for me to fight with illness so frequently. Every time I would say to myself, "Now no more energy is left, I have to surrender." But my heart never let me do that. It used to say to me, "You are the winner, you will not let any evil overpower yourself because the biggest power is always with you, GOD." And so again, I would get charged and regain energy to fight my illness.

By early morning when I didn't get relief, my mother asked my brother to take me to hospital. The doctor admitted me at once and examined my condition.

Dr. Ashish also joined in my treatment. Whenever he would come on a round to see me, he would sit with me for as much as 20 minutes and always tried to make me laugh with his funny jokes. He used to say with the people around, "I thought I should be properly dressed up because I am going to meet my heroine." The moment he would enter my room, he would say, "How am I looking, heroine? I know you would only praise your Dr. Vivek. After all he is tall, handsome and I stand nowhere. He is much smarter than me. He is your Salman Khan Bhai." Actually, I used to compare Dr. Vivek with Salman Khan and Dr. Ashish with Sharukh Khan. That is why, he used to pull my leg by showing himself as inferior when compared with Dr. Vivek.

When he would say all these things, I would start smiling, keeping all my pain aloof. This is the quality I believe all doctors should have.

Next day when Dr. Ashish came to see me, he examined my city scan report and told me that the lower lobe of my left lung is dead, due to which I was getting frequent infection.

Both the doctors discussed together and again kept me on antibiotics. Four antibiotics were going at a time on me but no significant improvement was seen in me. They included and excluded antibiotics but didn't get the expected improvement.

Later, when Dr. Vivek came on a round at night, he examined me and said that he was going to keep me on a very hard antibiotic MEROPENEM because light antibiotics were not working on me.

After the five days' course of that antibiotic also got completed, it didn't show significant improvement. There was improvement but not at a speed the doctors expected. My fever was also not subsiding. So, on the 12th when Dr. Ashish came on a round, he talked with me and my sister for a long time and told my sister that he suspected that I might have tuberculosis and I should go for a bronchoscopy test.

But I was scared, I thought him to be a new doctor. He didn't have experience, how will he perform this test on me? Everybody tried to convince me but I didn't listen to them. You can't imagine how I collected all information about him on the internet through my sister. I collected all information from his studies to all papers he published.

I cursed Dr. Vivek that how he could let a new doctor perform that test on me. I did not agree with that decision at all. When my sister saw my attitude, she got to know that nobody could change my decision. So, she decided that she would talk to Dr. Vivek over it.

She called on his number and told him everything. He told her that he would talk to me at night. When he came, I directly said to him, "I will not go with that test. I want Noida's best pulmonologist. He must have not treated a case like mine. My lung's location is not the same as in normal people."

At that he shouted on me and said, "You don't know his achievements. He has won 11 gold medals. He has performed this test on a six-month-old baby. He even made a person stand who was on his deathbed. He has performed this test on more than two hundred people and how did you think I will let you be touched by a person who is not an expert."

When he said that, I agreed to that proposal with closed eyes.

Now it had been fifteen days since I was in the hospital. My bronchoscopy was scheduled at 11. 30 am. I was afraid and left everything on Allah (God). They (the ward boy) took me to the ICU for the procedure.

Dr. Ashish was already present there. When he saw both my mummy and sister very disturbed, he allowed them inside the ICU room. My Mamu (Rizwaan) was also there.

It was a big thing that Dr. Ashish allowed all people who were with me inside the ICU room. I observed he had humanity. He knew my mum and sis had life in me and my bronchoscopy was riskier than that of others because I was so weak. Any mishappening could take my life. That is why, it was for their satisfaction that he allowed everyone inside, leaving other guardians out.

Dr. Ashish tried to anesthetise me through the nebuliser, but medicine was not reaching inside my lungs due to my inability to suck. At this, they both decided to give me anesthesia directly through that tube, in this way the medicine reached inside, and so Dr. Ashish could perform bronchoscopy procedure.

I was so afraid. It was not painful, but in between, my breath stopped for five to six seconds, my eyes filled with tears, both the doctors were trying to make me calm. Dr. Ashish kept on saying, "Don't cry, baby, the procedure is over." Although he was performing the test alone but in between he tried to keep me calm.

A strange thing I observed. When I was crying, I saw tears in Dr. Vivek's eyes as well. I don't know why but

I was very much attached to him since the first time I had met him. I trusted him a lot and it was he due to whom I had agreed for this procedure. God had developed my full confidence in him.

When everything was done, Dr. Vivek left me without informing me. I was feeling very angry at this act of him.

When my breath became normal, cough choked in my throat, Dr. Ashish did tapping in his own way and all cough came out. He stayed there in the ICU until I was normal.

At around 2 pm, I was shifted in the room and reports came two days later, but it didn't show any growth. Dr. Ashish told us that it might be because I had already been put on heavy antibiotics. I should have gone with the test before the medication going.

My both lungs were much relaxed than before, but my body temperature was not coming down. That became the big issue.

Next day when Dr. Ashish came on the round in the morning, he directly said that he was going to put me on tuberculosis medication, at this I argued with him, I said, "I will not take any medicine on mere assumption."

He said, "You just keep your treatment with you and let us do our treatment." He got angry on me. The same was said by Dr. Vivek when he came on a round.

Actually, I didn't want to take any medicine on just a doubt, because they didn't have any proof that I had tuberculosis. They were giving me tuberculosis medicine just because my fever was not coming down, and second thing was that my CRP rate was also very high.

Later Dr. Ashish changed my antibiotic. Now it was linox, it worked on me and my CRP rate came down. My CRP rate was 32 at the time of discharge. Now Dr. Vivek could put me on oral medication. It was the longest period I stayed in hospital, it was as many as 22 days long.

□

52
I Took Tuition for Accountancy

When I came back from hospital, I had tension about my exams. It was my second year and I had to give my all papers in order to complete my 12th.

I was not in a position to attend school regularly because I had been very weak due to frequent illness, but even then I decided I would give my paper somehow.

The teacher who was teaching me at school, Mr. Praful was a good accountancy teacher, but he never cooperated with me. I asked him many times to give me home tuition, so that my syllabus could be completed on time, at that he would everytime say, "Zeenat, from the next week I will come to teach you." But he never came and my time got wasted. So, when I came back from hospital, I didn't ask him and rather took tuition from another teacher, his name was Naveen Soni Mitra.

I got to know about him through an aunty. I started taking tuition from him from the beginning of December 2013.

He had complete command over his subject. He taught me very well. He always had solutions for my doubts. With his technique to teach accounts, my interest increased in this subject. His teaching was more efficient than that of Sameer Sir, maybe because he had previous experience in this area. He was in the teaching profession for many years. I was very much satisfied with his teaching.

During my classes, Parth used to come. He would stand next to my bed while I concentrated on numericals. His brain was so sharp that he could mug up all that the teacher orally taught me. One day he came. I don't know what had happened to him. He started speaking with my sir and sister, "Manni Bua is zero and Saba Bua is 100 percent because Saba Bua can walk and Manni Bua can't." And then again he spoke the same lines with me as well. It seemed from his face how desperate he was, he wanted to see me walk. His desire could be seen in his eyes filled with tears. He told me, "Manni Bua, now nobody will help you until you start learning to walk of your own." I never saw that desire even on my parents' face of my being independent in life, maybe they had got used to the situation, but from a small kid's face, it truly appeared how much he wanted me to walk.

Nobody in this world had ever spoken to me these practical lines which a small kid made me realise. He spoke to me the truth, although those lines contained the bitter truth, but these showed his love for me. What wrong had he said, he just wanted to see me like others? He made me realise a thing over which I was struggling since my birth. I always try to balance the difference between my life and normal people's life.

Naveen sir completed my syllabus within three months. Only revision was left, which he planned to do one month before the exams, which means in March, because after that I had to appear for exams in April. Unfortunately, I again got ill in the first week of March. The doctor once again admitted me on seeing my symptoms.

□

53
Hospitalisation Again

My brother Mazhar would never take a risk in my case. If I said I am having a difficulty in breathing, he would immediately prefer to take me to hospital. He was very caring towards me and I always pray to Allah that his caring nature should remain the same even in future. Nobody should change his mind.

Soon after, I was admitted. Next day, Dr. Ashish came and said, "How come Zeenat got admitted? Why didn't you tell me?" At this, my brother said, "Actually, doctor, everything has happened so suddenly that we couldn't inform you."

Dr. Ashish said, "Zeenat, you could have left a message on my number."

I said, "Doctor, I was unable to even hold the mobile."

Dr. Ashish said, "I can understand, baby. Yesterday Dr. Vivek called on my number and told me you are not well, that is why I have come to see you."

Then, after checking me properly, he said, "You took the right decision of admitting her. She needs prompt action," and then he left.

It was getting very difficult for my family to manage around two lakh rupees twice a year for my treatment, I myself would feel very bad, I didn't want my family to be overburdened due to my illness, but what could have I done? There was no control over my health issues.

I always try to get well with oral medication but I would become helpless when I start breathing heavily. In that case I needed fast absorption of medicine in my blood and that was only possible through IV and by proper care under doctors' observation.

My sister tried to get a health insurance policy for me so that our financial burden get lighter than before but letter after search she found out there is no such health insurance policy created by the govt. for people with chronic diseases. In our country policies are for those people who have least chances to get admitted in hospital. In simple words all gain is for govt. and insurance companies and whatever loss comes is to be bear by common people. Govt. should make amendments in their policies and rules to make India comfortably lived by everyone. If we see countries abroad the govt. there is more flexible for such people.

Dr. Ashish used to see me everyday in the hospital and whenever he would come, he would make me smile with his funny jokes.

Initially, I was placed on a combination of two antibiotics, but when it didn't work, Dr. Vivek again started MEROPENEM and soon after, my both lungs got cleared in just two days.

Dr. Vivek suggested my father to take me home and could give remaining doses of MEROPENEM from home since I was out of danger then. My CRP rate came down, it was 42 then. The CRP test is done to identify the level of infection in the body.

Dr. Vivek said so because he thought of keeping me in hospital unnecessary is notgood, and secondly, I could have secondary infection also. So, he said to my father, "Take her home. Why will you spend money unnecessarily on hospital charges. You can continue IV from home as well, and now she doesn't need special attention by the doctors."

At the time of discharge, when my sister checked the payment list, she noticed there were no charges on account of Dr. Ashish's visits, although he used to see me whenever he was on the round.

Later, I got to know he was a very generous person. He used to visit me at my home more often, and would sit next to me and share his good and bad. In fact, all people, whether from my family, school, all would collect their problems and seek solution from me. Even my principal, Mrs. Vandana Ma'am shared her talk with me. Sometimes, I would think if I was sitting with my principal or friend.

□

54

I Got a Writer in the Form of a Good Friend

I got discharged in the middle of March. Now only two weeks were left for my accountancy paper. I still remember its date. It was on 29th of March in 2014. I had tension as my revision was incomplete and Sir forgot to complete one chapter. I had cannula in my hand through which IV fluid was being administered.

I did not understand how I would turn the pages with the cannula on and hold the book over my stomach, but somehow I managed because I had to give the paper and Naveen Sir had also helped me in this. He told me, "I will hold the book, you just see and don't worry about the revision. I will do it in no time."

Two-three days after the discharge, my maid Tabussum said, "Appi, without your presence your bed doesn't look good and Parth used to come everyday and holding your pillow, he would say, "My Manni Bua, come soon."

I needed a person for 24 hours, that's why mummy kept that girl Tabussum for me. She used to do all household work including that of mine, except cooking. Actually, it was getting very difficult for my mother to handle everything alone, because of which need arose for a maid.

I needed a person for all time around me to turn my head, to move my hand, to change my position; for everything I needed a person. My life was not mine. I was living some other's life. There was no my control over my body. I had only control on my mind, on my thinking. I would think what I want, and there was no control of others on my thoughts.

Sometimes I had a feeling what this life is which you could not live in your own way. You have to take every step according to others. You can't live as per your desire. Over this, many times, I prayed to Allah (God) at night and every time I would get only one solution, that's 'KEEP PATIENCE'. Verily Allah is with those who keep patience.

So, whenever I supplicated deeply, I would feel calm and relaxed. My energy and hope from God would augment than before.

Now only one week was left for my examinations, and this time I couldn't make my siblings my writers because they belonged to the science field and in accountancy you need a proper writer, who has a little bit of knowledge about accounts. In accounts, you need to draw many different tables, like for balance sheet, cash book, journal, ledger, etc. How would I have dictated a person of some other stream, these were the issues. Secondly, what is needed to be considered was who would have taken care of me during the exam, if I needed to drink water or change my position. All these things I couldn't expect from a stranger who could act as my writer.

My tutor Naveen sir helped me the best way in this issue. He discussed my case with one of his students named Shweta. She was also a commerce student. He had full confidence in her that she would write my paper and would handle me as well during the paper.

One day, he brought her to my home to meet me, so that we both became familiar with each other and could clear our doubts.

We met. I found in her a very nice and helpful girl. She had the ability to handle me during exams. Sorry, I should replace the word 'ability' here with the word 'kindness'. She was a very kind girl and had a feeling for me. Nobody could do my work until or unless he/she is emotionally attached with me or had a feeling for me even if he/she has 100 years of experience in handling people like me.

The day of 29th of March came. My cannula was removed one week before the exams. I was feeling very relieved, and now my sister Erum also went with us for exams. She thought that after making my arrangements, she would leave the exam hall, but to my luck, when teachers over there saw my condition, they allowed my sister as well inside the hall.

I gave my paper very comfortably and came back home after dropping Shweta at her home. I really enjoyed this paper. I got all expected numericals. My paper went very good. Now my next paper, business studies was on the 19th of April. There was a big gap. When the date came, I took the same writer Shweta, and when we reached the centre, I found out that the date had been postponed. Now it was on the 4th of May. All my efforts went in vain. For a normal person, it doesn't matter much if his effort gets futile but in a person like me, there are lots of preparations involved.

Now on the next date, I went for the exam. I gave it very comfortably, and again got the expected questions. I was very happy because my both papers went well.

When, after my examination, I asked Naveen Sir whether I should give some money to my writer, at that he said, "Zeenat, don't even ask her about the money or else she will not write paper for you. See, all the people in this world are not the same. They are nice people. They don't help people for money."

Whenever people heard about the writer, they would ask me, "How much money did your writer take for writing your paper?" When they get 'no money' as my reply, they showed amazement because they believe some writers demand 20 to 30 thousand for writing a paper.

But she was a nice girl. In fact, her whole family was very helpful because nobody likes to leave their young girl with strange people, and her parents didn't know my parents personally but they still sent her just for me.

In a few days, we became good friends. She used to call me and I used to call her. Sometimes we did chatting on 'Whatsapp'.

□

55

It was Result Time

The NIOS result used to come in the first week of June. I was in my room. The result was to be declared at 12 noon. My eyes were fixed on the watch because I was very excited to see my result. My papers had gone very well. Unfortunately, when I got rady to check, I found that my internet was not working. It was showing some problem since morning.

Finally, in the evening, the internet connection was restored. So, I got the chance to check. When I entered my enrolment number, I found the result being shown as 'withheld'. All my excitement turned into tears. I knew it would involve a long procedure and who would take so much of pain of going to the NIOS so frequently.

Everyone in this world is so busy with his errands and too much expectation is not good from anyone because if he does not match up to your expectations, it hurts. So, always keep expectations from God because He alone could give you more than your expectations.

After a long effort, when my sister went to the NIOS, they informed her that I was getting unexpected marks in business studies. That's why, they didn't declare my result and wanted to meet me. Next week, when I went to the NIOS with my sister and Mamu, the team of teachers, including the director of the NIOS, came down near my car. Earlier they wanted me to give the paper again, when my sister explained to them my physical condition, and when they saw me with their own eyes, they just asked me a few questions and said to my sister that they would declare the result within two weeks. They then left just saying to me, 'Best of luck'.

My result came on the 16th of August. They declared my business studies result and I got 82 in it, but again a problem was faced. My accountancy result showed me absent although I had given it. I was heavily tensed. The moment one problem was solved, a new problem would occur. But I was not a small thing that could surrender so easily.

□

56
My Year Wasted

I was much tense because my accountancy result showed me absent. My sister and my cousin went many times to the NIOS to sort out things, but these government bodies are the worst bodies in the world. They just make you run from one counter to another but never come to any conclusion. They get money from the government but never give out even one-third of what they get.

When people from my family said that they couldn't do more in it because they (NIOS) didn't listen, I shared my problem with my principal, Mrs. Vandana Ma'am. She gave me an assurance that she would help me. First she sent the HOD and some teachers with the issue to the NIOS but when the problem didn't sort out, she went herself. Even then nothing good came out. So, finally at the end of 2014, I decided to fill the examination form again. I didn't want to waste my another year, although my principal was feeling sorry for me that I had to give my paper again and on the other side, she was feeling proud that I didn't lose hope and was ready to give the paper again.

My year 2014 was wasted in wait that they would declare my result someday, but they didn't. That's why I decided to give paper again in 2015.

□

57

I Got the Publisher for My Autobiography

There is a very interesting thing in my life that I haven't told you so far in any chapter. Now I want to share it with you. In the year 2011, I decided to write my autobiography, the first part of the one which you are reading now.

I wanted to share my life experience, my struggle to make my life better, my achievements and everything from my birth to the life I lived, to this world.

In that initiative, I got suitable suggestions from my principal. First I decided I would reveal my story as a fiction lived by a real person, but when I discussed it with my principal, she suggested me to write the autobiography. With this, people would be able to feel the real experience. This is what I did, I wrote THE REAL FIGHTER for this world so that they don't get scared of small things in their lives, rather they must fight. This book was my dream and I didn't want to confine my dream within a limited number of people, only within my family, teachers and friends, but I wanted it to get to the whole world.

Once it got completed, I wanted it to get it published. For that I needed to hunt for a publisher, which wasn't possible in my case, even writing a book wasn't a cup of tea for me but my heart repeatedly forced me to write. Although holding a pen was like climbing a mountain for me, but still I tried. Later when my fingers didn't support me, I started writing it on the computer.

Although it wasn't easy for me to move my fingers on the computer as well, but somehow I managed. During the course of writing, nobody helped me. It was all my hard work. Everyone in my family was busy. In fact, my sister used to think that my book wouldn't be published because autobiographies are written by famous people.

In spite of all this, I didn't lose hope and I did everything, lying down on the bed whatever I could do in getting my book published. I thought maybe our school's (Managing Trusty) Mrs. Shanam Chadha could help me in this, and from that, I made up my mind to meet her.

And so I started the process by leaving everything on Allah (God), our Creator because without His help, I couldn't be helped by anyone. If he didn't want my book go ahead, no power in this world could bring it out, but on the other hand, He says not to lose hope. I have the ability to make your dreams come true even in the last breath of your life.

Believing these lines, I never lost hope. I started mailing my principal every alternate days, requesting her to fix my appointment with Shanam Ma'am.

Finally, after a long effort, the day came. My appointment was fixed in the month of November. I met her. She gave me an assurance about my book getting published. She left everything on my principal and asked her that my book should get published by a good publisher, but the publisher they could find out was a struggling one.

I couldn't expect from her more than that because, as I told you before, keeping expectations from these worldly people is the biggest foolishness because they will never reach up to your expectations. If you really want to keep expectations from anyone, then it is no one but the supreme power. If you repeatedly ask Him something without fail, I am sure He will listen to you someday, even if that thing is not good for you, He carries the ability to make it good for you.

□

58

A Line That Pinched Me the Most

It was the month of February 2015, a time of changing season for me. In this time, I generally get ill. In the first week of this month, I had flu, and so, first I took oral medication and when it didn't work, I got hospitalised again.

Now my immunity was becoming very weak. That is why, I frequently got hospitalised. And it wasn't easy for my family to collect such a big amount of Rupees 2 lakh every year. I was also growing very tense with this, I was thinking how I will go with such a situation in the future. As I keep telling you since the beginning that at a particular phase of life, you become alone, nobody takes a stand for you and why they should, they have their own life, their likes and dislikes. I would never want to become a hurdle in my family's happiness.

I always want my siblings, when they get married, to enjoy their life. They should not waste their time in looking after me. I don't want to keep any expectations from them, rather I want to be independent in life, for which I have been struggling.

When I went to Bhardwaj Hospital with my Mamu (Irfaan Kerkhi), fortunately he had come to meet us and my brother was in office. So, he and my sister took me to hospital. Dr. Ashish was there. He examined me and found my pulse rates very high. He gave it a term (tachicardia) and suggested my sister to get me admitted. By that time, Dr. Vivek hadn't come.

When he came around 12 pm, both the doctors discussed and then put me on a combination of three antibiotics for a day.

Dr. Vivek came close to me before leaving and said, "Zeenat, I am going abroad today. Until my return, you will be completely under Dr. Ashish. I will be back in three days. My flight is tomorrow morning." Then immediately, Dr. Ajeet, who was there in the emergency room, said, "Doctor, the moment you entered, she started smiling more than before. Earlier, her smile happened to be dull, but now I can see a change in her smile."

At this, Dr. Vivek smiled and said, "You know, Zeenat, all mothers have made me Mogambo. They use to tell to their children to take the medicine or else Dr. Vivek will come." He said so and left.

Dr. Ashish was like a friend to me. There were no formalities with him. I could have said anything to him, but he never minded it. Initially, when I had to go for bronchoscopy, I did so much of investigation regarding his education with the help of my sister and when my sister shared this to him, he just said, "Zeenat, you thought me to be such a small thing, yaar I have won ten gold medals." I felt very embarrassed for this, although Dr. Vivek shouted on me when he got to know about the investigation and convinced me to go through the test as he was a genius doctor.

And in Dr. Vivek's case, I always find him in a hurry but then, I also had an attachment with him. Although he gave limited time, yet I never minded it because in this world, people have different ways of living their life.

When I was shifted to the room, Dr. Ashish came on a round again. He said to me, "Enjoy, darling, watch the TV, nothing has happened, you will be alright soon." I like one thing in him. When he would come in contact with his patients, he could maintain his facial expression and try to make them feel calm by telling them that everything is fine, even though the patient is not well. Sometimes I liked this, sometimes I didn't because I would think if I am not feeling well, how come everything would be fine? And in Dr. Vivek's case, his facial expression would remain the same until he heard entry of enough air into my left lung.

At night, Dr. Vivek came to see me last before leaving abroad. When he reachedjust close to the door and was ready to leave after checking me, I felt bad I didn't want him to go but I didn't say it to him.

I said immediately, "Doctor, how will I contact if I need you?" He said, leaving the room, "You message me on the Whatsapp whenever you need me and I will be in contact with Dr. Ashish. So, don't worry." He smiled and left.

My medicines were going, the same medicines that the two doctors had prescribed me, but I was not feeling well still. My condition went worse the next day. Dr. Vivek had left. Dr. Ashish had also left for home by that time. I asked my mother to confirm the hospital authorities if he is there in the hospital, but he wasn't. It felt like somebody had pressed my both lungs and I couldn't resist. I was unable to take a breath. I started crying, I couldn't hold up myself. The doctor on duty came. He was Dr. Ishtiyaq. I asked him to call Dr. Vivek. I started cursing him, "O God, please get his flight cancelled." I was in immense pain and if he was around me, I would feel comfortable. I had already developed so much of confidence in him.

My mother was turning me here and there on the bed, but I was not getting any relief. I was afraid that my doctor was out of the country, and if my condition got deteriorated, who would handle me? It was he who knew everything in my case. I cried so much that my both eyes were swollen. I missed Dr. Vivek so much.

When Dr. Ishtiyaq saw me crying, he said to my Mom to keep me on one side in a tilted position. In that position, I got some relief. My maid Rubina wiped my tears. When the doctor saw me a little calm, he said, "I can't bring your Dr. Vivek, but don't worry, all doctors are here. If needed, Dr. Bhardwaj will also join in your treatment."

But the problem wasn't that. Even Dr. Ashish was trying his best. He used to see me thrice a day and sit for a long time next to me. He would always try to make me laugh. Sometimes he would call me from his home in order to know my condition. What more can you expect from a doctor? It was my confidence which by Allah was on Dr. Vivek. So, I started crying in trouble. At that time. I couldn't use my energy to fight illness. His presence around me would assure me that I would be alright soon. Maybe he didn't know all this, but it was true. Sometimes, I would get surprised why this was so, but later, I accepted it with the belief that it was God's will.

Although later in life, I didn't find him the same as before. He had changed a lot, but his medicine still worked. Sometimes it would hurt me a lot because I was unable to find the reason behind it.

Now let us come to the main point. Next day, Dr. Ashish came on their rounds. When he got to know everything from my sister that I was crying the day before, he said to me with smile, "Arrey yaar, don't take tension, you will be alright by tomorrow and I will discharge you before your Dr. Vivek comes." At this, a big smile came on my face. I said, "Okay, doctor, and when are you going to let me meet Vidushi ma'am?" He said, "Soon."

Dr. Vidushi was his wife. She was a dermatologist. He checked me and left.

Next day, he was on leave but I was surprised when I saw him. He came especially for me. Although he had many patients admitted in the hospital but he didn't go to them. He was in a hurry. He came inside and said, "See, Zeenat, whom have I brought for you?" It was his wife Vidushi. She talked to me for a while and then they left.

Next day, in the morning, when Dr. Ashish came to me, I said, "Doctor, you are very lucky, your wife is very pretty."

Dr. Ashish said, "Oh, you had such a handsome munda like me standing before you and you were looking at her."

I started laughing loudly and said, "Yes, yes, doctor." He then checked me and found a slow improvement. There was a very little entry of the air in my both lungs. When the physiotherapist would come, she would do tapping in her own way. It was how I could release some cough but again my lungs would become tight. Now I could see tension on Dr. Ashish's face, although he would try to appear calm before me. But that day, I could see tension on his face. My Mom said to him, "Doctor, please change her antibiotics because she is not feeling well." At this, he said, "Aunty, we can't change antibiotics so frequently. Now it's been only three days. They will work. Don't worry." He said and went out to add one more medicine.

I can't tell you how difficult it was for me to cough out. Every time with my remaining effort, I would bring it out to my throat and then push it out. Again in a few minutes, the condition of my lungs would become the same.

The fourth day when he came to check me, I said, "Doctor, I don't know why I am not feeling better. The sequence has remained the same. When I cough out, I get some relief but again my condition reverses to the same condition. Did you talk to Dr. Vivek? He told me that both of you are in contact." He said, "No, darling. Okay wait, let me call him." When he tried his number, it was switched off. He said, "Dear, don't worry, you'll be alright by tomorrow and I will discharge you before your Dr. Vivek comes."

He always tries to make me laugh and then again after checking me, he spoke another joke to me. He said, "Zeenat, do you know if you were alright, you would be only my girlfriend." I laughed at this comment, but somewhere in my heart, it pinched me a lot. This line made me realise in my whole life that somewhere I am less than others. I wanted to cry but couldn't because I didn't want to show my pain to the worldly people, as they don't have the ability to remove anyone's pain. I always prefer to cry in front of my creator.

□

59

I Gave Accountancy Paper Again

Once again I got fever. My IV course was completed but my fever did not subside. I went for a re-check-up. Both doctors checked me and found my lungs clear. I asked Dr. Vivek if I needed any mechanism on a regular basis for removing cough. He told me that he didn't have any idea about it and he would let me know after confirming it from Dr. Ashish. The same moment he called him up and confirmed.

Dr. Ashish told him that I didn't need any mechanism. Physical effort is enough for removing the cough or that, he even explained steps to my Mom and sister.

After that, the issue was my fever, which was not completely overcome. Dr. Vivek recommended a urine test. When I went with the report along with my sister and cousin Farhan, he found that my UTI was higher than the normal. He again prescribed me a medicine amecacine for seven more days through IV. The same pharmacist used to come twice a day.

I can't explain you how much irritated I was with the regular antibiotics but the doctors couldn't do anything in it. They had to give me antibiotics to fight with the illness, because my immunity was very low, a small flu would turn into a big infection.

Now one day, Dr. Ashish came to meet me. By this time, my IV course had been completed. He was a very nice person. Being a doctor, his schedule was very tight but then also he would take out time for me. He used to come and sit next to me and then we both talked. He would share all his college-time experiences, his achievements and everything. Sometimes I would laugh, sometimes I would listen to his talk very sincerely.

After having lunch, he again said a joke. He said, "Zeenat, I always try to make my wife feel insecure. I use to say to her that my patient Zeenat is so beautiful and you shouldn't take *panga* with me." I always laugh at his jokes. The good thing in him was that he always found the way to make me laugh. Nobody could stay upset under his influence.

Now only one month was left for my exams as it was on 17th of April. This time I didn't prepare much. I thought I would prepare only that much so that I could clear my 12th. My health wasn't supporting me in order to pay more attention to my studies.

I called Naveen Sir, my accountancy teacher and said, "Sir, please give me time whenever you are free. I just need a revision so that I could recapitulate the chapters." He was also very cooperative. He never said no to me. I always found him whenever I was in need.

He again asked the same writer. Shweta to write my paper because she knew everything about me and he was confident that she would take care of me during the exam. When he confirmed it from her, he found her busy during that period but the amazing thing was she got ready to write my paper. She gave the least priority to other things as compared to my need.

We had fear whether they will accept her as my writer because we didn't prepare the writer's application till then. Actually that year, they had started a new criterion for writer's application. They (NIOS) wanted a written proof from the writer's school that he or she is an existing student of their school and so no school was ready to make any document like that. I even asked my own school because I had a firm confidence that they would definitely help me, but they denied. My principal told my father that she couldn't help him in it. My last hope was my school but as I told you, everyone has their own point of view of thinking, although it wasn't a big thing. The NIOS just wanted a formality that was needed to be fulfilled.

But nobody helped me and I have no regret for that. I thought, "If Allah doesn't want me to give paper this year, I have no problem, I will appear for the exam next year."

But at the last moment, just one day before my exam, Naveen sir called on my Mom's number and told her that Zeenat would give the exam. He would make that document from my coaching centre, showing that the writer is taking coaching from his centre and giving exams privately. It will have the stamp of centre.

He was very nice. He helped me and prepared that document.

My writer, Shweta also cooperated a lot. She told me, "Zeenat, don't doubt about me. I will write your paper in any case." She left her own paper and went with me to write my paper.

17th April came. Both Shweta and my sister. Erum went with me. This time my centre was at KV School, Ghaziabad. I was lying down in the car. My sister went inside for making my arrangements. She explained my condition to the school authorities, but initially they were very strict until they saw me. They all were arguing that they would provide their own writer, but the moment they saw me, everything was changed in a blink of the eye. Their attitude became totally different. They gave me a special treatment. We were astonished to see that. It was all God's blessing on me that my problems got solved every time.

I went inside and gave my paper happily. There was no hurdle as people used to make it. Shweta was also accepted as my writer. We reached home by 9:30 pm after dropping Shweta at her home.

Both Shweta and Naveen Sir cooperated with me a lot in this. My mummy gave him his tuition fee but he didn't accept it. He told my Mom that he would not take the money and if she asked him again, he would stop coming. Even Shweta didn't take her share.

I would say that this world exists as of now just because such people live on this earth.

My result came in the first week of June. I scored 49 out of 100. At the time of paper, I couldn't attempt all questions. I lost 18 marks' questions. So, I thought it might have been the reason behind my poor marks. Sir asked me to send my paper for a re-check, because he expected 60 even after losing 18 marks' questions, but I told Sir that it was enough for me that I had cleared and I didn't want any further processing. Who would take the pain as everyone was busy?

□

60

A Drastic Change

You must be thinking what change would have taken place in my life. In your thought, you must have only one thing that is good. I would say you can see it from either end, good one or bad one.

Now I will break your suspense. Do you remember that in my first edition, I had told you about a line, which was being said by me to my Mom that I will stay in my own home? These spoken words were fully realised by God (Allah). A plot about 112 m was drawn in my name in a draw released by the Noida Authority in Sector 122, Noida. Its construction was completed by 2012, and so it was given away on rent by my father.

On June 16th, 2015, we left Sector 37 and shifted 7 km away to Sector 122 in my own home. The home I talked about to my Mom in the year 2008, and it came out in physical form in the year 2015, when we actually started living in it.

Later I realised it was what I had wished. Allah made it true. A house with the name ZEENAT ARA engraved on its nameplate came true. I wanted to say thanks to Allah, but instead of saying anything, I started crying. There were no words on my lips except "O my Allah, you are the greatest among all. There is no limit of your blessing on your humans but even then people are so unthankful to you." Tears were continuously coming out of my eyes.

Since it was drawn in my name in Noida Authority, my father got it registered in my name for my future use.

Now you must be thinking that everything was going as per my wish, then how could it have a bad side too. Now it was the most concerning issue.

First of all, I want to tell you one thing that I never expected to leave Sector 37 someday and I always wanted my father to purchase a home in Sector 37 or around the area, but he didn't. He purchased a flat in Sector 82 when my elder brother Azhar was ill. It was his last wish to have a home in Noida. He wanted that we should settle down in Noida permanently, and my father had already purchased a plot in Kanpur. It was his favourite place. So, he had made up his mind to finally settle in Kanpur just after the completion of children's education. But he sold out the plot when he purchased a flat in Noida.

Now you must know why I wanted to stay in Sector 37 or the area around it. Because, as I have told you, I was suffering from SMA (spinal muscular atrophy), which affects the voluntary muscles of the body and the muscles start to degenerate with the passage of time, due to which the immunity of the patient becomes low, and so these patients catch flu more often, and their flu converts into infection and that normal infection converts into a deadly pneumonia. When pneumonia is diagnosed, it becomes very difficult for such patients to fight with the illness. It feels like somebody has forced them to climb up a mountain, and even after the rigorous efforts by doctors, they sometimes leave the world.

So, my readers, that was the reason why I didn't want to leave Sector 37. My doctors, my hospital, everything was at a distance of five minutes from there. I could get medical assistance in emergency in just a few minutes, and the infection would not get time to convert itself into pneumonia. And the second thing was we had 25 years of standing in this sector. We had many good neighbours over there who could come to our help in need even in the middle of the night. Creating such type of bonding would take time in Sector 122.

So, my readers, this medical assistance was a big issue, due to which I never wanted to leave that area. Since I knew my limitations, I tried to get myself prepared in advance.

I suggest to all those who are suffering from this problem or who are not, may have children with this problem should consider this thing also, mainly in order to increase the children's lifespan.

In my case, it didn't happen, but I tried my best because in the sight of Allah, one is best who tries and keeps hope even to the last breath. The same I did and I will keep trying until I win. I have never been unthankful for what He has provided me with, but sometimes there are other issues linked with it; for that He never said in his statement in the Qur'an not to try to make your condition better. In fact, he says, "I will help those who help themselves to improve their condition."

□

61

Smiling Eyes didn't Let the Distraught Heart Show its Pain

When we shifted on 16th June, it was the afternoon time. I was taken up by my cousin Asad inside the new house at around 3 pm. During my whole journey in the car from Sector 37 to Sector 122, tears were continuously coming out. They didn't stop until I reached Sector 122. I was feeling like I am losing something which I couldn't get ever again in life.

Actually, I don't know what is in me that I use to get attached with things and people very soon, and when they hurt me or go away from me, it becomes very painful for me. So, it was my love for people and things in Sector 37 that was coming out of my eyes in the form of tears. Some people there were so good that they usually took out time from their busy schedule in order to come and meet me, like Dadi (Daya) about whom I have told you in my first edition, Mushtaq uncle's family and many more people and yes, specially all my teachers who were living close to that Sector including Negi Ma'am. In that sector, there was hope that Negi Ma'am could come if I need her. She could come to meet me walking, which was not possible here in Sector 122. My DM Sir was also living in Sector 27, close to that Sector. You will get to know how I met him later because by that time, I hadn't met him.

And, one more special person, without seeing him, my morning wouldn't start. It was my rabbit Parth. I missed him so much that my morning would get spoiled everyday. Actually, he used to visit me every morning before going to school. He would remove my blanket and would say, "Bua, look who has come, it's your gudda (doll), Now I am going as I am getting late." Just by saying this, he would leave and my eyes would open in a beautiful morning. Actually my rabbit would make my morning beautiful and here I didn't have anyone who could bring a spark in my dull morning. I went through the times when I felt I could run away from there and reach the place which would bring a real smile on my face directly from the heart but due to inability of my limbs, I couldn't go anywhere.

I want to share an experience of my life when I realised the importance of my limbs the most. Before that I used to manage everything without its need just by using my brain, the master of the whole body, but when I shifted here, everything became easily accessible for me, since now in my new house, my room was at the ground floor. I could enjoy more, you know it was my desire since long back when I was a small child that I could live on the ground floor. That was fulfilled in this new house. Here things became very easy for me, like I could go anywhere around my house without a long procedure like to arrange someone who could bring me down the floor very carefully and then bring my heavy wheelchair down as well. Nothing like that was here. No issues like this were here. But it is true, you get the things when you are not in a state to enjoy them fully. I got this pleasure but I never felt like enjoying it. It was like you have your favourite food kept within your reach, but when you are ready to eat it, you don't find its taste the same. It tastes differently. The same had happened to me. I got what I wished for since long back, but when I actually tried to open it and stepped into it, I didn't find it the same.

Here I had the feasibility to go anywhere, but unfortunately, I was left with limited options to go anywhere, like I told you, here I had been separated from people known to me who could take a stand when I needed them. I had the surrounding but I didn't have the people of my choice in that surrounding to whom I could go in my wheelchair. People over here were very rude. They didn't like to interact with others and the most amazing and noticeable thing about them was they wouldn't bother if the neighbour in their adjacent house would die in need. They would never come to help.

Although in a normal case or with normal people, they can adjust anywhere without much adjustments, but in my case, I required special attention, advance arrangements because with me, emergency could occur anytime, but I had no pleasure like that over here. For that I had to go seven km away. I can't tell you I went through the days when I felt very bad from inside. I had the feeling to cry all the time. I would go outside the house but nowhere I would find peace. In that period, I missed the importance of my limbs the most. If I had my limbs, I could go where my heart sought. I could break the barrier and reach Sector 37. Not only I, but also my mother, sister and brother, all had the same feeling. They knew it wouldn't be convenient for me.

I would sometimes try to convey to my father but when I didn't get the expected response, I stopped convincing him in a belief that it was Allah's plan. I thought my father was old now. I should not give him trouble by making him shift from one place to another. If I can't do anything for him, I should not give him trouble. There might be a possibility he might have some personal problem. But, one thing I never let go, it was hope from my Creator. Maybe someday Allah puts me in a position that I could purchase my own house around Sector 37. I just accepted it for the time being as Allah's will.

□

62

The Best Opportunity I Received from Allah in Doing Something in Favour of My Bua

Now, my readers, things became easily accessible to me, but it created a limitation as well. From the area I had been shifted, every necessity was at a big distance that was needed to be considered with the families having patients like me.

For a normal family, it wouldn't be an issue, but with me, it was a big issue. Gradually, I started realising these limitations. My mother couldn't go anywhere leaving me alone with the maid because all markets and everything else were at a long distance from my home. It would take her as many as 4 hours to go and do all shopping, and to leave me alone for 4 hours with a maid in a place where nobody might emerge in need couldn't be a good decision. So, my Mom was trapped with me in house. She couldn't go anywhere until she kept a responsible person around me, due to which her freedom was restricted. Actually, in that period, my sister was doing M.Sc. in microbiology from Jamia University. So, she used to stay away in Okhla for 6 days and get time to stay at home only on Friday and my brother was supposed to be in office the whole day. He got time only after 9 in the evening. My father, as I have told you earlier, was out of station for most of the time as it was the part of his job.

So, whenever she got any of these family members at home, she would go out to meet our needs.

Sometimes, I would feel very bad for this as my Mom's freedom was restricted just because of me. She was in her old age and in your old age, you need to be around more people known to you, whether they're relatives or long-time neighbours with whom you have a good bonding. You expect to spend time with them at least once a day, but no liberty like this was available with my Mom here. She could go neither to Sector 37 nor any other place for a change, leaving me alone with the maid for long hours.

I always wanted to give my parents a good care in their old age. You must have remembered Ayesha (my Bua). She was like an aliment (oxygen) for me, without which human life is not possible. Now I know you must be wondering and thinking of this a stupid thought that if she was an important aliment for me without which human's life is not imaginable, then how come I am alive. By this statement I mean to say or try to convey to you is to always believe in a simple maxim: everything is following the order of supreme power, everything is in His control. So, when I lost my important aliment, He (god) might have changed my mechanism t live. He might have designed my life in this way that I ddn't need her anymore as oxygen to live my remaining life. He can change all mechanisms and form a new system for human existence because He is the only designer of this world.

So, coming to the main point, I wanted to do something for my Bua, who had given all her life in upbringing me but Allah didn't give me this opportunity.

After her death, I realised that Allah had blessed me with the best opportunity in doing something in her favour. Now I am going to tell you one more important thing about this life through which I will be able to explain it more properly. This world is temporary, not permanent. God has sent us here to test our ability to finally receive the best award (the permanent world). He has sent us to perform as many good deeds as we can possibly do, against the complexity of this world. What I mean to say by complexity of this world is that this world will always try to mislead you from the right direction because it is full of desires, and this desire can lead you to both directions: right or wrong. Sometimes we opt to achieve this desire by the way this fake world shows, not the way the Designer of this world asked for. He asks us to do good deeds, be a gentle human with a firm belief in his power, if we follow his edict, He will make us that much stronger to pass this temporary world's test to be finally rewarded with the permanent world.

So, the best opportunity I was given by Allah of doing something in the favour of my Bua was that I could offer prayers for her to get her enter the permanent world, that is Jannat (heaven).

She was a great lady, her good deeds in this world were more than enough for her to be rewarded with the best, but the love and affection sent by people of this world in the form of prayers must have increased somewhere her grades in good deeds.

So, I pray in her favour and nothing could be the best for her more than this.

And so, I want to do something for my parents as well so as to keep them happy. It is the duty of all people to do whatever they can do for their parents because it is the most precious thing we have been blessed with by Him (God). You can get everything second time in this world except this pleasure, especially Mom. My Mom had sacrificed all her freedom and spent all days and nights with me in a place where no one was much familiar to her. She too could have left me or taken me in our native place where most of our relatives stayed but she didn't do anything like that, because she knew at least here in this Sector, I could have the connectivity with the people who can help me go up or achieve something, although it would take time, but at least here was the possibility.

This sacrifice could be done by none else but by my Mom in my favour. Whenever I pray Allah now, I ask Him to make me independent so that I could do something for my parents to keep them happy.

□

63

I Received My Lucky Award by DM Sir

It was the time after Eid when I received a call from the Hindustan newspaper that I had been selected for the award given by DM of Noida, Mr. Nagendra Pratap Singh to 11 women for an act of bravery in the district of Noida (Gautam Budh Nagar).

I have told you that I was very upset because all my friends, teachers and others were left behind in Sector 37. This news brought a slight smile on my sad face. I forgot everything for a while. I just thought about receiving the award.

The day approached. I still remember its date. It was 25th of July, 2015. I can't forget this date ever in my life because it was on this day that I met a person who gave a new direction to my life.

I went with my Mom, sister and Bilkis Aunty to Sector 6 where I was to be awarded. When I reached there and the anchor started calling up all awardees one by one, my sister felt that my achievement was nothing in front of those who would have been awarded. She thought why they had called me, just to give me pain because my physical condition was zero as compared to those awardees. They all were physically fit.

As compared to them. I had many limitations. I needed to change my neck position more often. The neck rest on which my neck rested would start putting pressure on my neck if I kept it there for a longer period.

And second thing, I had a curvature in my back, which starts aching a lot if I sit over a longer period of time.

This was the reason that my sister thought so. She didn't want to see me in pain unnecessarily.

You can't believe when the anchor announced my name, everyone stood up in ovation and the roar of applause was so loud that I too could hear it clearly. Actually, later in life, I lost the power of hearing from one ear.

It was unbelievable for my sister as well as for the audience and awardees present there. The anchor requested all to give the same respect to other awardees as well.

At that moment, I had tears in my eyes. Allah had again made me win over others, who were physically more capable than me. My sister took me on the stage with the help of others. Now I was to be awarded by the person who had the ability to read my heart. He was my DM Sir, Mr. Nagendra Pratap Singh. I don't want to describe him in a long statement or else it will take time for you to make out his importance in my life, I would just say that he was an angel for me, whom Allah had sent saying to his heart, "Go, Zeenat needs you." No one has the power over himself when Allah does something through him.

Allah has sent many angels in my life in the form of different people when I needed them for doing various tasks in my favour, and the most amazing thing was that I used to observe in them that they had lost this quality just after having performed their tasks. Angels are being put inside people for just a small period of time. Once the work is done they are being taken off.

When DM Sir passed the award in my hand, though I wasn't able to hold it, I had a different feeling in my heart, I didn't want to go away from him. I heard a voice from my heart, which had a regret for not being able to speak a word with him. Maybe it was from Allah's side who has developed a desire in me to meet him because Allah had already planned to put in him an angel for my help.

After the award-giving ceremony got over, DM Sir gave his speech. In his speech, he talked about female empowerment and said, "I am against plucking of flowers but when I gave those flowers to Zeenat, I felt that these flowers are going in the right hands."

After the event got over, I asked the anchor to send my message to the DM that I wanted to meet him. But she forgot and I saw DM Sir was ready to leave. I felt a big regret in my heart that I couldn't meet him but when I saw him turning to my side, I was very happy. He himself was coming to meet me.

When Sir came, he said, "Your book is written very beautifully. I will definitely read the whole book and then let you know." After that, I clicked a photo with him. He was in a hurry, so he left the venue soon after.

When all audience, anchor and awardees saw him leaving me, they surrounded me like I am a celebrity and then started clicking pics with me.

□

64

Spent Four Hours Sitting Next to DM of Noida (A Proud Moment for Me)

I was very happy for the award I received from the DM Sir, but deep inside my eyes, there was a pool of tears which I kept on trying from letting it to break the barrier to burst out of my eyes.

As, my readers, I told you in the beginning that there is no value of your tears (pain) in this world because nobody tries to find out the reason behind your sadness, but if you have a smile on your face, they will have insecurity to know the fundaa (formula) behind it. So, I suggest you never to show your pain to others who have narrow hearts. Show them your smiling face.

By saying this, I don't mean to include all people in this category. There are people who have capability to absorb millions of people into their hearts.

On the one hand, I was happy with the award I received and on the other, I had regret that I was unable to do marketing for my book (The Real Fighter) because everyone was busy, including my principal (Mrs. Vandana Sharma). My book was my dream (a massage to this world I wanted to spread) but it wasn't possible just by lying down on bed. I needed a support, which I was not getting and along with it, I wasn't feeling good in the area I had been shifted to. It was a very isolated place. I would feel very lonely here.

I was left with two options: either to cry over my sorrows or to keep faith in Allah. I selected the second one. I would always find positivity in all situations and never give preference to negativity. With belief and patience, I went ahead.

One week later, I went to my school. I wanted to show my award to Vandana Ma'am and others at the school. When I reached her office, she was very happy to see me. I told her everything about the event, but when I said that DM Sir had told me that he would meet me again after reading my book, she replied back, "Beta, it's not easy, he is the DM, he might have said but it's very very difficult." At this, I said to her, "Ma'am, I don't know about him but I will definitely meet him."

When I came back home, I messaged the Hindustan newspaper asking them to provide me DM Sir's office number. The moment I received the number, I called on it. A person spoke up from the other side. I explained to him how I had met DM Sir and told him that I want to meet him again. I called him many times regarding this, but I never got a satisfactory response. Every time he would give me some excuses. When I got fed up with this, I shouted on him. I told him, "What do you expect from a girl, who couldn't hold the phone herself, to call you many times without any result. Please tell him I want to talk to him."

Next day he called on my number and said that DM Sir wanted to talk to me. When DM Sir came on line, I said, "Sir, I want to meet you." He said, "Fine, you can come tomorrow at 11:30 am at my office." Then I said, "Sir, how did you find the book?" He said "Nice, but you come first, then I will let you know in detail."

I was very happy. I called on Vandana Ma'am's number and told her that my appointment had been fixed with the DM. Now suggest me what all I should ask from him. She was amazed that I had done what I said. She couldn't believe that DM Sir was on line with me. She herself was very happy that I could so easily be connected with him. She said, "Beta, ask him about marketing your book."

The day had come and I got ready to go to DM Sir's office with my father and sister.

You can't believe, I received such a big welcome at his residence. I had a feeling that I am being welcomed like a queen. Everybody was waiting for me outsides before I reached. They said to all the people who had come before me to wait outside, DM sir wanted Zeenat in first.

When I entered his office, he said to my sister, "Don't stop her there, bring her next to my chair." He said, "I have read your book. You have explained things very nicely, especially I appreciate you for not having any regret from Allah for you to have been born like this. You are a very brave girl."

After that, he said to his secretary, "Today Zeenat is the VVIP for me. Just send in the people sitting outside one by one. I will attend them also side by side.

That moment I felt so proud that I was sitting just next to DM Sir. I was blessed that I was getting a VIP treatment from the owner of the district. It was like I was seeing a dream. He was a true human. I felt in him humanity. This is one quality God wants in his people in order to make them the king of both the worlds (this temporary world and the world hereafter the permanent world). DM Sir had that quality. That is why, God made him the king (DM). Allah gives the best of this world to those people who have the ability to utilise it properly. He never gives to those the power and the pleasure who have an attitude to give little importance to others in their comparison. In fact, they don't know there is no word like attitude in this world. The people who say they have attitude, they are actually the victims of a disorder called inferiority complex. How could a word like this be developed in this world when the designer of this whole universe never shows the attitude to his people. He has the greatest right to show attitude to his people that they are zero until he makes them 100. If Allah hates any word the most, that is 'attitude' and if He likes any word the most, that is 'humanity' and he does the same to His people.

So, now coming to the main point, my readers, after that, people started to come inside his office with their queries. They were amazed to see me sitting next to him. Sir introduced me as his friend to all and side by side he informed everyone that his friend had written her autobiography (The Real Fighter). It's a motivational book, everyone must read it once in their life.

He asked me, "What favour do you want from me, Zeenat?" I told him directly, "Sir, I want to be independent in life. I want to bear my expenditure myself, because at one point of life, you are left alone. No one takes a stand for you, not even your parents and in my case, I would need a minimum of Rs. 1.5 lakh for my treatment within one year as I need hospitalization in severe condition. So, if possible, please help me promote my book."

At this, my father said, "I don't know why she takes tension? We are always with her." DM sir replied back, "I don't think she has said something wrong. Life doesn't go barely with emotions."

When he said this, I had frozen tears in my eyes which I tried hard to stop from melting out of my eyes. He had spoken the word that was trapped inside my heart.

In between, he sometimes would get busy with others, and when he saw me, he would say, "Don't think I am not listening to you. Speak up, I am listening to you as well and if your father and sister are getting late, let them go. I will not drop you, you haven't eaten anything yet." After that, he asked my sister what he should order for me. What could she easily eat? After that he ordered juice as per my convenience. We all had juice. My father was looking at his watch. He was getting late for his office work. So, I asked DM Sir to give us permission to leave. I got my pictures clicked with him and during this, he was adjusting my wheelchair's position by himself. I asked him, "Sir, please, my sister will do that." At this, he replied back to me, "Am I not a human? Can't I do that?" It was such a big proud moment for me.

□

65

I was Selected by DM Sir as Chief Guest for the Launch of His Book *Tejasvani*

I was very happy. I was being invited by DM Sir to call him any time I was in need. I used to talk to him through Whatsapp and phone. He said to me during my meeting with him, "I will sponsor your studies. Just find out an appropriate college and course for yourself."

These words spoken by him increased my hope towards studies. Now I started seeing dreams of doing best, the fashion designing course. I even discussed it with one of my cousins (Ruksana Bajji), whom I used to believe a good guide. She has the ability to guide the person towards the right direction where he/she can get the best output.

Earlier, she said to me to go for English honours. She even tried to enrol me in the same course through online admission in DU through distance learning, but, she couldn't do so because my practical paper in home science could not be cleared as I was admitted in hospital at that time.

When I let her know about what DM Sir had told me, still she insisted on me to go for the same course. She said to me, "You have a writing skill. You can improve your vocabulary with it and make book-writing your profession." I said, "Ok Bajji, I will do that." But somewhere in my heart, I always wanted to do fashion designing. I used to sketch dresses on Paint in computer as I have told you. Later, in my life, my finger movement became low, due to which I couldn't draw on paper.

At this, she said, "You can't go for any course this year until you have not cleared your practical exam. First try to talk to DM Sir to help you in arranging something so that you could give your paper again. After that, you will be able to do some course."

I messaged to Sir that I wanted to meet him regarding my practical exams. He replied back, "Beta, send somebody on your behalf with your issue because I will be busy in a meeting." I understood that he didn't want me to wait outside his office unnecessarily. So, my brother went to meet him with my issue. After getting over with his meeting, he called my brother in and offered him sweets. He treated my brother same as his friend's brother.

He asked my brother to write down a note and give it to the person sitting outside and at the same time, he called the city magistrate, discussed my issue with her. On that, she said that she had the same issue on which she was working currently.

He said, "Keep Zeenat's issue at top priority. She is very close to me."

And you can't believe, my readers, everything was done within one month. I gave my paper and received the result also.

Once my result was out, I asked my sister to go to AMITY in order to talk to them, if they could take me in a designing course. Along with it, what facilities they could provide in my case?

After collecting all information, she came back with only one option that I should do English honours in distance education. For that they could only provide CDs for lectures. They didn't have any disabled-friendly facility.

After this, I didn't ask her to do any more research because she was also busy in her studies and I couldn't expect more than this from her. I felt very bad and helpless inside. I thought if I could at least move my body parts, I wouldn't have needed anyone's help. I could do all by myself.

I was overburdened with my pain inside my heart but I never let it overpower me, to make it stop bringing a smile on my face. I decided I would keep patience. If nobody could see pain behind my smiling face, then Allah would definitely see it one day.

Now my sister got busy in her studies and I couldn't get admission even in English honours that year.

I was very sad and sobbed for some time and then accepted it as Allah's plan.

A few days later, I received a call from DM Sir. He said, "Zeenat, can you come tomorrow at 9:30 am?" He told me the reason also but since I had a hearing problem, I couldn't hear exactly what he was saying.

I reached there 10 minutes late with my brother and sister. He said to me, "Today you are 10 minutes late, Zeenat." Actually, Sir liked my punctuality. When I met him second time in his office, he appreciated it a lot. He told everyone that he had called me at 11:30 am and I was right there at sharp 11:30 am.

So, now coming to the main point, I saw a bundle of books kept on the table just in front of me. It was the book *Tejasvani* written by DM Sir. He wanted it to be launched by me. He had called me as the chief guest for his book launch. It was again a proud moment for me. I was sitting just next to DM Sir and his other side was the SSP, Dr. Pitender Singh.

It was such a big moment for me. It was for the first time in my life that I was being called as the chief guest, that too for launching DM's book. He wrote this book on female empowerment and their safety. It was a nice book.

After the book launch, news reporters started gathering around him and put cross questions in front of him. In all his interview, he just spoke about my book (The Real Fighter).

Although it was the occasion to speak about his book, but he gave preference to my book.

He spoke in his interview, "It's a must-read book, which motivates all generations in all possible ways." I noticed in him a quality every time how smartly he tackled all questions coming his way. He spoke things logically. In all his words, he always made a sense which benefitted an individual and society together. I saw this quality in him while he was dealing with others. This quality must have made him crack the IAS examinations, the most advanced and difficult.

It was a proud moment for me to sit next to an intelligent person, my DM Sir. My pride redoubled when I was helped by him, whenever I was in need throughout the time I was there next to him.

□

66

My Endeavour to Keep Myself Happy

When I was called up by DM Sir for his book launch, everyone known to me read this news in newspapers. They all congratulated me in their own way and praised me for my talent that I had impressed DM Sir. They believed, not all but a few of them, that I can't go far in life but when they saw the extent of his inclination to my side, they became helpless to believe that I must have something in me which brought him close to me, that finally he became my friend.

This happiness wasn't enough for me to keep myself happy for 24 hours, I wanted to get the result (increase in sale of my book) but the issue was, when my book was not in market, how its sale could be increased. Nobody had the time to bring it in market. My school at least helped to bring my written material into a book form. I couldn't force them further. It was their own duty to do best in my favour according their bright student, a top priority. They knew it well that I wanted to be independent in life even being in this condition. So, they should respect my intention and help me proceed ahead in life. I don't mean to criticise them. They did what they felt good. Everyone has his own way of thinking and preoccupations and I never take it in a negative way. It's just my feeling that comes directly from my heart over which there is none of my control. I always appreciate their support for me. But here I can't control my writing to explain my feeling. We can control our feelings to cross the boundaries of our lips but when you start writing something, your brain automatically starts supporting your fingers' movements. Our brain gives order to all our voluntary actions involved (hand, legs, etc.), though you can control your feelings coming out from your heart to your lips. Your brain can't force your lips.

So, I was surrounded with issues. I wanted to utilise my 24 hours in such a way that I could get some benefit out of it in my favour. Since in that year, I couldn't enrol myself in any institution, I had ample time to utilise it any way, but I wanted to spend it in the right direction, to find out someone who could help me take my book ahead (market) and that couldn't be possible sitting at home. My school could do that only. They had my book kept in school, and second most important thing was, I wouldn't feel good in the sector I had been shifted. So, I thought maybe going to school twice a week could bring some change in my mood. As it is, wherever I would have been, I would not have stopped going to school completely. I would have always kept myself connected with it, whatever the means.

So, finally, I decided to talk to Vandana Ma'am (principal) over it. One day, I went to school, it was September 2015. I discussed this issue with her with a better understanding, I said to her, "Ma'am, my life is becoming blank sitting at home. If possible, please let me do some administrative work at school that suits my physical ability. In this way, I can come to school twice a week and my interaction level wouldn't be limited." At this, she said, "Beta, give me some time to think over and since you are at the ground floor now, you should go out and enjoy yourself." I replied back, "Until you have not the surroundings of your choice, you can't enjoy anywhere."

After that, I came back home with my sister. Now she had to go to Jamia for her studies. She used to stay six days there out of seven and my brother used to go to office and my father used to stay at home for just three days: Sunday,

Monday and Tuesday, he used to go back to Kanpur where he used to work in some leather company.

Now can you imagine that only my Mom and me were left at home, at a place where we had not much interaction with others. If we would need any help at noontime, nobody would have emerged out from their homes. It was just like that days passed and we were not able to enjoy a single moment.

When I didn't get any response from Vandana Ma'am for many days, I messaged her, "Ma'am, I can sit in control room and monitor all the cameras fitted in all classes. She replied back, "Zeenat, come on this day." I was very happy. Now I will get a chance to interact with more people but, on the other side, I was tense about my Mom. She would be left alone at home.

But my readers, mother is only a relation who could even put her life at stake for the sake of her children's happiness. My Mom said to me, "Don't think about me, I can live. You just join the school if you are happy."

One Friday, my sister came home. It was her off day from her college. So, I took her with me to school. I met the Principal Ma'am. She was very happy. She made me meet people who would guide me how I could join them. She told me one more thing. She said, "You will be joining us as a volunteer. There will be no compulsion on your duty. You sit in the control room as per your wish. The moment you feel you are tired, you can go in the medical room and take rest. We have arranged this to maintain your interaction level."

I came back home happily. At least I got something. It was better than nothing. Actually I wanted to do some job at school. That would support my physical limitation and my school could only provide a job seeing my condition because they themselves run a school for physically abled children. Anyways, I saw the positive thing in it and let go the negativity.

I discussed it with Abbu (father). He said to me, "How will you go twice a week? It wouldn't be manageable." I told him that my school bus would pick me on the days I have to go. They only want me to bring an attendant who can hold my head in the bus in her lap." He consented to this.

It was very difficult to search a lady who could go with me to school twice a week. My Mom talked to many ladies but their charges were very high. Actually, my Mom had no idea about maids working here. That was one reason they were showing their importance. Finally, she found a lady who was ready to go to school with me on reasonable rates. I went to school five times in two months. After that the days started becoming colder because December was about to start within two weeks. This was my effort to keep myself happy.

□

67

I Received an Award for Excellence in Creativity

As I have told you that I went to school five times in two months, I would have gone on more occasions, but I would get tired so much. The bus, which used to run on my sector route, used to take as much as one hour to reach my sector (122). Before joining school, I had thought it would take same time as it took to reach Sector 37, but later I realised it when I actually started going to school.

In spite of all these hurdles, I couldn't restrict my life within the boundaries of my home because I was left with two options: either to suffer a long journey or to sit at home, since I couldn't go back to Sector 37.

I can't tell you how painful it was being in bus for long hours, especially for a girl like me, although the maid used to lie down me on the seat and put my head in her lap. She used to hold me tightly but even then, when bus ran over uneven roads, it would jump wildly. With that my back would jump over the seat. That would hurt me a lot. And with that, you can imagine how many times my back must have been taking jerks in one hour. It would give so much of pain in my back, but I preferred to get happiness after bearing pain rather to get relief to receive sadness at the end.

Now the temperature started decreasing as it was middle of November and I contacted flu due to weather change.

I immediately messaged Dr. Vivek about my symptoms. He replied back some medicines to me. With those medicines, I recovered within five days. This time my illness wasn't that severe that I would need to be hospitalised.

One good thing I got in this house was that my health was going well. Allah made things easier for me. The frequency of illness became less as compared to before. He knew it wouldn't be easy for me from here to often go to the doctors who attended me. So, he made the arrangements in my favour, I didn't need to go to doctors more often. Allah loves me. In fact, He loves all humanity. He takes care of my happiness, whether these worldly people do so or not.

Although I didn't like to stay in this sector a second, but I can't deny the truth that God has made this house very lucky for my health. In fact, this house was lucky for my whole family because, as I have told you before, we got it in a draw released by the Noida Authority in my name, Zeenat Ara.

So, when I recovered, I received a call from Jyoti Ma'am from my school. She told me that I would be getting the best achievers' award for excellence in creativity on 5th of December, 2015 in FICCI Auditorium, Delhi by People First Foundation. She told me that as only one week was left, I should not go out in between because I had to be there to receive my award. I thought how I could receive the award in case I fell ill.

Now only two days were left to go for 5th of December. On 3rd of December, my phone started ringing and I was in a deep sleep. Generally I switch off my phone before going to sleep, but that day I forgot to switch it off. It was ringing for long and when I asked my Mom to give it to me, I saw it was DM Sir calling me. By the time I could hold up the phone, the call got disconnected. Then after some time, I again received a call from him. This time my phone was with me and I picked it up. He said to me, "Zeenat, I have sponsored your studies with the U.P. government.

Now you search for a good college and take admission. It's a gift for you from my side on Disabled Day." That day was 3rd of December, World Disabled Day. I was very happy but the problem was the process involved in that. I had already wasted my one year in this but didn't get any result. What he could have done in this was to give orders on, the procedure involved after that was to be tackled by us.

The same day some reporters from India 24/7 news channel came to my home to take my interview. DM Sir had asked them to visit me. He explained my story to many reporters and told them that they should meet me.

I gave my interview. It went awesome. After that I gave many interviews and my story was published in many newspapers, I got a good recognition among people. Now the whole district knew Zeenat Ara. DM Sir had fulfilled his promise. He publicised me a lot. Now if my book would have been in market, it would have sold well.

Now I was getting appreciation from everywhere. People used to treat me like a celebrity. Wherever I would go, people would gather around me and show their desire to click pics with me.

It was all Allah's blessings which were showering on me one by one. These blessings were making my happiness double before the day I would get the award for excellence in creativity. I was very happy the night before. I asked someone to apply nail paint on my nails because at that time, my sister was in Jamia.

The day had come and this time I went with my parents without my siblings. It was the first time when my sister didn't accompany me. We reached the venue, FICCI auditorium sharp at 5.30 pm.

It was such a big event for me. There had come big achievers, who all had achieved a lot in their lives. When my turn came to receive the award, two people took my wheelchair up the stage. While taking it up, its one side got dismantled. Actually, I had my award in my mind. So

I forgot to tell them about my wheelchair arrangements. On seeing me, the anchor and the minister who gave me the award forgot everything. They praised my spirit to do more in life without fearing about the hurdles. The anchor gave me compliment, "You are very beautiful and so is your smile." I was very happy. All celebrities present there clicked pictures with me. I met Karan Oberoi (singer), Prachi Telhan, former netball captain. She herself came to me and talked about me. Until that time, I didn't know her. She too praised me. She said, "Zeenat, you are too beautiful." I found her very nice by nature. She stood just by me for as long as I was there.

While receiving the award with my wheelchair having one side missing, I felt very embarrassed because my Principal was also present there on the stage and I respect her a lot. With my wheelchair not having one side would have spoiled her image but nothing like that had happened. Everyone considered me only and the things associated with me became invisible to them.

□

68

My Hope Got a Way

At the event, I met many big personalities. They were very impressed with me and took my number. Dharmender Sir, the Chairman of PEOPLE FIRST FOUNDATION showed his desire to get me associated with his organisation.

I was ready to leave the venue before it got over. Parul, who had come to take my interview before the event, insisted my parents to stay till the event got over, but my parents told her they couldn't because they had to leave for Gonda the next day as they had an engagement in their relation. So, she brought both the anchor and the singer out from ongoing event to click pictures with me. They both were very nice. The anchor stopped anchoring and the singer left his performance in middle and came out to specially meet me.

Next day on 6th December in the morning, I received a call from DM Sir. He said to me, "How are you, Zeenat? Is there any cure for your problem?" I replied to him, "I am good, Sir. According to me, what I have searched on the net, there is no cure." At this, he said, "Anyway, I have talked to the CMO to suggest you some good doctor, so that your medical re-examination could be done and any cure could be found out."

Once the call was disconnected, tears were streaming down my eyes. Although its cure is not yet found, yet research abroad is going on some drugs. There are only two techniques: stem-cell therapy and gene-editing therapy, which show some hope.

Stem-cell therapy is the use of stem cells to treat or prevent a disease or condition. Bone marrow transplant is the most widely used stem-cell therapy, but some therapies derive it from the umbilical cord. Blood cells are also in use. And gene therapy is a form of therapy that involves inserting one or more corrective genes, that have been designed in the laboratory, into the genetic material of a patient's cells to cure a genetic disease.

I did all the research about my problem. When I had read about these techniques, I always wanted to go through them, but since now my parents were old, I didn't show them this desire. I didn't want to give them pain in their old age. They have run here and there a lot for my treatment when I was child.

But when DM Sir said that, it showed a ray of hope. It wasn't like that my lost hope had awakened suddenly with DM Sir saying so. I always had hope from my Allah. I never get disappointed by Him. It was just with his saying that my hope got a way to be realised.

With my eyes full of tears, I thanked Allah a ton. I gave this news to everyone at home. They all were very happy.

Same day in the evening, I left for engagement with my parents and brother. My sister was in Jamia. She had exams during that period.

We were supposed to leave for home on 16th of December. My father and brother had come much before us, that is on 10th. They left on the scheduled date. I was there with my Mom. The engagement ceremony was performed. Now, all the relatives invited us one by one. When I went to my middle Mamu's house, all my cousins had also come there, including Hena about whom I have told you in my first part. She had flu and was sneezing badly. When I saw this, I wanted to keep her out of the room because, as I have told you, I could catch infection very soon and that infection could turn into a severe pneumonia, if not treated on time. But I didn't say anything to her. I just said, "Keep yourself away from me, please." Actually, people don't take things in the right way. They always make out negative intentions out of such things. So, I didn't say her any further. I didn't want her to get annoyed.

□

69

Three Days' Hospitalisation

What I was afraid of came true. When she left, I too started having trouble in my throat. I had pain in it. With that I knew I would have infection. I immediately asked my Mom to give me nebulisation with budasole. When I didn't get any relief, I asked my Mom to call my sister and tell her to call Dr. Vivek and ask him medicine as per my symptoms. Actually, I wasn't in a condition to even hold my cell or else I would have messaged him on Whatsapp of my own.

When I couldn't hold it up myself and my condition started deteriorating continuously, I decided I would not stay there a single moment more. Everyone including my Mom said, "Let's consult a doctor here first. Once the condition is normal, we will plan to go back." But I couldn't take the risk with my delicate condition. My case wasn't a normal one that any doctor could have handled, nor could I allow a doctor from a small town to spoil my case.

My fever was increasing rapidly. It touched 100.6°F. It was no more under control. This was the sign that my infection level was shooting up. I was murmuring, "How will I reach Noida?" I regretted why I took the decision to leave Noida in the changing weather, when I was already aware of my limitations. Suddenly, I disappeared into a thought. I used to consider the distance between sectors 122 and 37 (where my doctor and hospital were situated) very huge and used to think how I would reach there in emergency, but being 567 km away from my basic need made me believe that 7 km was very small distance. In Noida, I could have reached there in half-an-hour, while it was big distance when seen from the point of emergency.

The second thing was that my doctors knew my history. They knew what steps should be taken and at what level of the case. Any new doctor would have taken time to first do investigation in his or her own way. Only then he or she could have come to a conclusion. I couldn't wait till that time to get my condition worse, that my own doctors would find it hard to control it. I was crying badly and praying to Allah, "Please make me reach the spot where you have provided me (shifa) cure."

When my Mom saw tears in my eyes, she knew something was wrong because she knew her daughter never broke down so easily. She then called my brother's friend, Ikram to make online reservation. Once the call was connected, he gave the phone to my brother Mazher. As they were on the way to Bhangad, they had planned to go for some outing, but when my mother asked him for immediate reservation, he got to know that something was wrong. He suggested Ikram to go back from there. Their outing got spoiled just because of me. He called Mom again and asked her to tell him everything clearly. At this, she told him about my health. He emphasised her to bring me by car as soon as possible. He then contacted my father who was in Kanpur and told him as well, "Mummy is bringing Manni from Basti by car. You just accompany them and bring her directly to Noida or else I will go there by car." My brother cares a lot for me. He always tries to take the best decision in my case.

So, the same day, we left for Kanpur. My Mamu accompanied us for the journey and he went back after leaving us there. I stayed there one night at the house of one of my father's friends. Actually, I didn't want to stay there.

I wanted to go back straight and Baba (my father's friend) too suggested me the same. He said, "If you have even a slight discomfort, you should go back right away because to consult any doctor here will be a foolish idea." But since I was taking medicine which Dr. Vivek had told my sister, my condition was under control.

We left for Noida next early morning. My parents admitted me in Bhardwaj Hospital, Sector 29, Noida.

Dr. Ashish (my pulmonologist) examined me immediately. He said, "What happened, Zeenat?" I told him everything. At this, he said to my father, "Uncle, you did the right thing to bring her here on time because she takes time to recover." He did all tests including the CRP (C-Reactive Protein). After that, I was shifted to a private room. I took a long breath and felt relaxed. Allah had sent me to hospital on time. I held up my hand in front of Allah and thanked Him for He never let more tears flow out of my eyes. He always answers to my prayers sooner or later.

In between, Dr. Ashish entered the room. Immediately I stopped praying. I never do prayers in front of people. At that time, I was alone in the room. My Mom too had gone out to buy medicine. Since Dr. Ashish had entered the room, I stopped talking to Allah because I prefer to pray when I am alone.

Dr. Ashish was very nice. He had already examined me in the emergency room, but again he came to meet me after I had been shifted to the private room. He would treat me just like a friend. There was no formality of doctor and patient between our relation. I asked him if he had informed Dr. Vivek. He said to me, "Yes, Zeenat, he is busy somewhere in his family. Don't worry, he has told me that he will come to see you soon, at around 4 pm."

As I have told you before, my readers, that Allah had developed my confidence in him, so his presence meant a lot to me to recover. Allah (God) sent him in my life at the time when I was stuck between life and death. Allah gave his hand as support to me to completely enter the life again. It was the time when I was admitted first time, in the year 2012. I was very critical, Dr. Bhardwaj, under whom my treatment was going, put me on good medication, but it wasn't working, and unfortunately, he had to go somewhere urgently due to which he gave me under Dr. Vivek. He came at night to see me. He found me too critical to recover. With his entry in my room, I felt something unusual. Although I was not able to open my eyes completely as I was in a half-conscious state, I could see with dizzy eyes a different grace in his face, a strong force around him which I never observed in him later in life. It was from my Creator (God) who filled my heart with love for him. Allah transformed him into an angel and put him in my service. His involvement in my case wasn't a coincidence, but it was a plan from the supreme power to make him a source throughout my life to live longer. He could have made anybody the source but he selected him for this opportunity for taking a good care of me. I was very confused when this thing happened to me for the first time in my life. I started to like him more than Salman Khan. He became my first and last crush.

After that, Allah (God) put him in my heart firmly as a big confidante that no force except Allah Himself could throw him out of my heart. I didn't tell you this, my readers, earlier because I was very confused about all these and didn't reach any conclusion till then. Later, with the passage of time, with my continued prayer to Allah, He solved this riddle. He made me realise that He had sent him in my life by giving cure in his hands and in order to make it more effective, He developed love and confidence for him in my heart. I always want to see him happy in his married life.

Now coming to the main point, I waited for him many hours after Dr. Ashish left. I was feeling very bad and was very angry on him. He had never been so careless towards me before, now I was seeing some changed in him earlier he used to be very quick in my case and would respond in a blink, but nothing like that was now, may be he started thinking that I am internally more strong than he use to think.... Such thoughts made a bunch in my mind, which made me more confuse. He wasn't like that before. At around 8 pm, Dr. Ajeet (duty doctor) came on round. He asked me if Dr. Vivek had come on a round to check me. I told him 'not yet'. The same moment he called him up letting him know that I had been admitted under him in room number 204.

In just five minutes, he came, stood next to me and said, "What happened to my Gudia?" I said annoyingly, "Why did you come so late? Didn't Dr. Ashish tell you that I have been admitted? If he were not there, what would have happened to me?" He said, "I am so sorry. I didn't know the room number. This will never happen from the next time." After that, he checked me and saw my report. My CRP was very high at 120. He chuckled, "You never score less than 100."

They put me on a combination of three antibiotics: Augmentin, monocef and vancomycin. This time I wasn't that serious and was being treated on time.

Next day, Dr. Ashish came to see me at the usual time. He took a round at 10 am. Whenever he would come to check me. He would give me some time. So, when he came, I told him everything about my meeting with DM Sir and told him how he keeps his profession away while meeting me. He is such a nice person. He has humanity in him. He said to me in response, "Zeenat, he is a very soft-hearted man and you are blessed that he gives you priority over others because it's not easy for any of us to talk to him so freely. A normal person has to think twice before saying a word to him. You are very lucky that he gives preference to you. He loves you a lot."

The same day I messaged DM Sir that I have been shifted to hospital safely. He didn't reply. I got to know that he must be busy in some meeting. When Dr. Vivek came to see me at night, he usually came on the round from 9.30 pm to 11 pm. He used to come in between anytime and in the morning, he used to come around 12 and Dr. Ashish used to come in the evening at around 4 pm. So, when he came just after checking me, he told me, "Your CMO has called me." I was shocked. I asked him, "What did he say?" He replied back, "He said that it's DM's order to find out how Zeenat is feeling." I said, "What did you say then?" He said, "I told him she is feeling well."

When he left, I thought that I was okay for DM Sir, not to reply. He directly wanted to know about my condition from the doctor. It was such a big privilege for me that the owner of the district was so much concerned about my health.

Now it had been two days since I was in hospital. This time I had the feeling that I would recover soon and would be discharged within two-three days. Now Dr. Ashish came on the round. That day he was looking very smart and so I gave him compliment, "Doctor, you are looking very smart." He said smilingly, "Ooh, don't tell a lie. For you only Dr. Vivek is smart. I know you like him so much." I too started smiling with amazement. I asked him with a mild smile, "Doctor, why do you think so? I always praise you too." He said with a smile, "I saw his name in your book everywhere." I said, "I hadn't met you till that time. That's why, you were missing in my first book."

When he went away, I felt very guilty. I felt very bad. I don't like to hurt anyone. I thought why he thinks so. I respect both of them equally. In fact, I appreciate him for his quality that he has humanity. Being a very good specialist, I have seen him talking to a poor man with the same respect and regards as with other people. With his this attitude, I myself didn't understand his capability when I had to go for bronchoscopy first under him. He was so nice that he said to me, "Zeenat, in case you need any medical consultation, I can visit you at your home. You don't need to visit me here." But whenever I used to go for a check-up, if needed, I would go to him as well. He was a generous person. Even in my family, if somebody needed him, he would try to come. He would treat my family as his own family.

I would find him always there whenever I needed him. That's why, Allah has blessed him with the most intelligent and pettiest wife.

And in Dr. Vivek's case, he too was very caring towards me, although his way of showing his care towards me was different. He was very quiet and hardworking, and the most important thing, he was the luckiest person. Allah selected him out of the whole world to replace Salman Khan from my heart, although he didn't have all the qualities which I want in my dream man. But as I have told you, my readers, everything is in the hands of Allah. He can do anything if He wants. If he had put him in my heart, I couldn't remove him even if I wanted, because he has planned it that way, and His planning is always meant for the benefit of his humans. He sends people or things in your life for some reason. There is always some plan behind everything he does with you. So, just keep patience and faith in Him to see the result.

The second day nurse again took my blood sample for CRP and it's result came the same day. Now my CRP was 39, but Dr. Vivek told my Mom that he couldn't discharge me at that stage. He couldn't take risk and wanted to keep me one more day.

So, I stayed there one more day. When my fever settled down, both the doctors discussed together and came to a conclusion to discharge on oral suspension.

□

70

Again Got the Chance to Sit Next to DM Sir

On 5th of January, 2016, I again got the privilege to sit next to DM Sir. He called me in his office to know where the process had reached in my treatment and studies. When I entered his office, he asked my sister, "Bring her here next to me. Her place is here." So, my sister placed my wheelchair next to his chair. Then he asked about my studies. I said to him, "Nothing much has been done, Sir. No college is ready to take me in fashion designing course seeing my requirements. I couldn't attend college regularly since I get ill very often and need teachers' proper attention and above all, no private college is yet disabled-friendly." These were the issues which I discussed with him. In between, a reporter (Devika) present there spoke up, "You can go for NIIFT also." At that, my sister said, "She needs to clear the paper first for that." DM Sir said then, "That is not an issue for her, she can clear that." When I heard that, I felt very good. DM Sir was showing his confidence in me. He was very proud of me. Even my family never showed such a big confidence in me, who used to see me all the time, and DM Sir got to know my ability in just one go. I also respect him as my parent.

Devika spoke up again. She said, "In fashion designing, you need to go to various markets in search of various fabrics and it wouldn't be feasible for you." At this, DM Sir said to me, "Zeenat, why don't you go for mass communication? You have the capability to become the best anchor. You speak nicely and Irfaan will help you to train."

Irfaan was in Channel One news. When DM Sir gave him the responsibility, he said "Don't worry, Zeenat, I will make you the world's best anchor and I myself will deliver all lectures or provide you with video at your home. I will take your classes and you don't need to come to the studio. I will come to your home."

Although I didn't have interest in mass communication because I knew my limitations, but since DM Sir had said so, I thought he must have seen some quality in me for that.

So, I got ready to enrol myself in that course.

After that, Sir said to me, "The CMO was telling me that your problem is incurable?" I said, "It's true, Sir, but I didn't lose hope. Everything is possible anytime." He said, "True." And that very moment, he called the CMO and said, "I want you to send a doctor, who has a good reputation in the AIIMS with Zeenat." He replied from the other side, "Sir, there is no cure for her problem and her family will have to go to AIIMS." At that, Sir said, "Okay, but at least we can try. A small improvement will give her a big gain and her family will go with her and a doctor will go with her as well." Just saying this, Sir kept the receiver down.

Few people in this world are like DM Sir. He is a great human who saw my problem from my perspective. That is why, he had the desire to get me at least some improvement in my problem and the other person was trying to find no hope in my case in order not to give pain to himself.

Now you can see the difference between two thoughts. Your thought changes the action and your action gives you the result. So, what I am trying to say is if the thought of the CMO would have been the same as that of DM Sir, I would have definitely got a good result.

Actually, when DM Sir had given me the news first time that he had talked to the CMO about my problem, I went to meet him personally, but he treated me indifferently. I felt very bad. I tried to say this to DM Sir in just taking a common example. I didn't say this to him directly because nobody can change with an external force (pressure by someone). Only their inner force (own try) can change them.

Sir even asked me many times, "What happened, Zeenat? Tell me frankly." But I said, "Nothing, Sir."

DM Sir said to my sister, "Find out the treatment anywhere in India. Whatever the amount is needed will be paid by the government."

What more he could say than this. He could only give the orders and the process involved ahead had to be followed by other people. Had the people been so active as DM Sir was, I am sure some solution would have come out. In that situation also, I had belief in my Supreme Power. He will definitely give me everything. To make DM Sir my friend was the assurance by God that He will make me reach greater heights. I was blessed, everyone has a dream to at least share two words with the DM of the district and Allah blessed me with this to share unlimited words with DM. It wasn't a small thing.

After that, the cameraman was all set to shoot my interview with DM Sir. I asked my sister to wipe my face. At that, Irfaan sir said to my sister, "No need, she is beautiful." I told him, "Do you know my Principal used to make my hair before giving any interview." At that, DM Sir gave me compliment, "You are already beautiful. You don't need to do anything." Then my sister went away. I gave a superb interview with DM Sir.

It was my experience from the end of 2012 till the beginning of 2016. It might be a possibility, my readers, that I may not be able to take you again in my world due to severity of my disease that might increase in future, but you never know what Allah may have planned. Where our power to think stops, Allah starts blessing us from there.

And a big thanks to DM Sir, Nagendra Prasad Singh, who came in my life like sun and gave it a beautiful morning.

□□□